CW01390791

Making Christ Visible

Robert Paterson

Copyright © 2018 Robert M E Paterson.
All rights reserved.
Published by Robert Paterson.
ISBN 978-0-244-75612-3

Most of the biblical quotations in this book are from
The Revised English Bible
Oxford and Cambridge University Presses, 1989

Cover photo
Obama Family at the Christ the Redeemer, Rio de Janeiro, 2011

Foreword

Who is this book for?

Anyone looking for ways to communicate a vital message about making Christ visible in his disciples, and for something to provoke them to think about the revolutionary demands and consequences of discipleship. It's hoped that the book will also make sense to anyone giving thoughtful consideration to the Christian faith.

What is the central message and purpose of this book?

In the face of decline the Church is dogged by strategies to equip Christians for ministry; this has led to an internalised approach to being a Christian disciple and to the meaning of Church. It's impossible to get out of this mentality without asking what being a Christian is about, and what the Church is for; ultimately, asking how Christians can make Christ visible.

What makes this book distinctive?

It raises both basic and new issues, questions some assumptions and challenges dumbed-down and pietistic theology and practice. One reader commented on my *'innate curiosity that leads me to ask how things work and why they sometimes don't work'.*

It's loaded with 47 years of experience in ministry with ordinary people, making, nurturing and sustaining disciples; and of being a church leader with international experience at a critical moment in the history of Christendom, convinced that the future for the Church lies in the quality of life demonstrated by Christ's disciples.

I am most grateful to those who have read the book for me and made immensely useful suggestions.

The book is dedicated to Pauline Anne, a very wise guide.

Enjoy!

+ Robert.

What people are saying about Making Christ Visible

This book is packed with a lifetime of vision, passion, experience and wisdom. Robert wants to help each of us live our lives as disciples of Christ, making him visible in our words and actions. The church is the fifth gospel, the only bible most people read, and this book will inspire and resource all of us to be better disciples in our world today. I commend it to you with enthusiasm.

Mark Russell, Chief Executive, Church Army

Following Jesus isn't easy – it is simply the best thing any of us can do. It is our amazing privilege to help people see Jesus Christ, and come to know Him. This is true for everyone. It's not about being religious, it's about becoming friends of Jesus Christ, and seeking to live his way in the world, in the power of the Holy Spirit, to the glory of God the Father. This book will help us both to be and to make disciples.

The Most Revd Dr John Sentamu, Archbishop of York

Robert's love of the Lord, of Scripture and of George Herbert shine through page after page. It's a lovely book; refreshing, helpful and challenging by turn. I found the reflection on discipleship, witness, ministry and royal priesthood as refreshing as iced water on a hot day. There are excellent reflections on Bible, on teaching and on church growth, and many lovely turns of phrase, typical of Robert's preaching style but even better when written down - and coming to a pulpit near me any Sunday to come ...

Andie Brown, Archdeacon of Man

A most stimulating book, casting new light on what discipleship is all about: I am certain that readers will find it both helpful and challenging. There are so many little gems here, quotations from a wide range of authors and a winsome way of writing. I am so glad of the emphasis on stepping into and becoming part of the story, which reminds me of the Ignatian exercises, and also of the need for disciples to embody holiness.
I hope that the book will be widely read and thank Robert for sharing so much of his own experience of discipleship.

Arthur Howells, Church in Wales

While many leaders have not quite understood Jesus' command to make disciples here is a bishop who has heard it clearly. His passion to be obedient makes him challenge the church in a robust way to eschew light Christianity and follow the Master's instructions.

Geoff Pearson, former Bishop of Lancaster

Robert's masterly, yet easily readable work stresses the need for the church to focus on the discipleship to which all Christians are called, at a time when it is inclined to be more concerned with specific needs and ministries. The biblical support for his thesis is presented with great clarity. Nurture is an important word here: it is made clear that the disciple has a duty to nurture others in their faith, and similarly to accept the care of others in an interdependence that leads to growth. And there is so much more too! I warmly recommend this book.

Dr Alan Wakely, Former Secretary of the Central Readers' Council

Bishop Robert's theme is that 'Christianity does not appear on people's radar any more', so the challenge is to nurture disciples not merely make converts. Every chapter contains thoughtful, scholarly and in depth study of selected Bible passages, enlightened by a wide range of literature. He cuts decisively across current debates about the various roles and status of lay people and clergy. Throughout is the plea for disciples to be learning about their faith as the first disciples did from Jesus and being enabled to live it in their own spheres and communities rather than being sucked into endless churchy activities that keep the institution going.

Christine McMullen, for 'The Reader'

A splendid production. I liked its direct style and very much admire the way it is written with such clarity.

Dr Robert McCloy

Contents

Robert Paterson

Robert is a Celt: born in Wales of Scots and Welsh ancestry, Robert was educated at King Henry VIII School in Coventry, then studied Theology and English and trained for ministry at St John's College Durham University, where he became Van Mildert Scholar in Divinity. His postgraduate thesis was in catechesis.

Robert was ordained in Manchester and subsequently served for 33 years in Wales, mainly in parish ministry and at national and international levels as Principal Officer of the Church in Wales Council for Mission and Ministry. In 2006 he became Chaplain to the Archbishop of York.

From 2002 to 2009 Robert chaired the Steering Group of the Anglican Primates' international working group, *'Theological Education for the Anglican Communion'*, he co-founded the Four Nations Liturgical Group and was involved in ecumenical relations at national and local level. He co-chaired two international Anglican - Lutheran symposia on the diaconate, and has published and lectured on preaching, worship, mission and ministry.

From 2008 to 2016 Robert was Bishop of the Isle of Man, one of the ancient dioceses of the British Isles; he chaired the Central Readers' Council for England and Wales and was a member of numerous other national church bodies. As Bishop of Sodor and Man* he was a full member of Tynwald Court, the oldest continuous parliament in the world. He is now an honorary assistant bishop in the Dioceses of Worcester and of Hereford.

Robert is married to Pauline and they have a son, two daughters and two grandsons; he used to row, and enjoys walking, cycling, music, the theatre, fiddling with clocks and messing about in boats.

The title 'Sodor' derives from the late-10th to mid-12th centuries when the Hebrides, or Sudreys, were united in one diocese under Norse influence. More recently it became the island home of Thomas the Tank Engine.

1 Called to make Christ visible

I don't agree with stickers on the back of cars: for me they invite accusations of hypocrisy. A fish symbol on my car would merely alert the driver behind to how badly the car in front is being driven. *'Little Princess on board'* is a terrifying prediction of serious trouble ahead - in more ways than one! My pet hate is *'Jesus of Nazareth is looking for joiners'*. I get the pun (of sorts) but the one thing Jesus isn't looking for, if the Gospels are to be believed, is joiners.

'Biblically the real challenge for the church is to make disciples (i.e., those who are actively and consciously following the way of Jesus), not to make converts (those who take a tentative first step toward Jesus).'[1]

Jesus calls disciples, Christians who make Christ visible. It is time to put discipleship back onto the top of the Church's common agenda and to clarify our thinking about discipleship and ministry. Disciples are converts but not all converts are disciples. Converts are those who have been changed; disciples also change the world. Ministers help and sustain disciples; ministers are disciples but not all disciples are ministers.

Many good things are happening today in Christian lives and through the Church the world-over. The Church is one of the most precious gifts of God, the bride of Christ, a means of glory. However, there are signs that can discourage us, and we are foolish to ignore them. In the Global North a financial crisis still lurks around and threatens voluntary associations like churches, the average age of our congregations is steadily increasing, and some of our ministers are in poor spirits. Callum Brown, in trying to identify the principal causes of the decline in British church attendance since the mid-1960's[2] identified the loss of what he called 'discursive Christianity', by which he meant that people in general are not aware of the Church or of Christian belief and practice in their daily lives and conversation; the Christian way doesn't appear on people's radar. Furthermore, in a recent survey in England,[3] 60% of the population said they believed Jesus existed, 22% believed he is a mythical character, and 18% didn't know. About half of the population believed Jesus was spiritual, loving or peaceful. This picture, taken from a different angle, confirms that our society is losing discursive Christianity.

In contrast, a real sign of hope is that most people in the street who know a practising Christian take a more positive attitude to the faith.

If there is to be any reversal of this downward trend of five decades, there has to be change. Change should be relatively easy to effect at the level of **externals** - organisational change, liturgical change, and so on, though churches can be conservative, so change even at this level can be a challenge, and the slow pace of change can be debilitating. It is more difficult to effect change at the next level of our **values** - sharing with others what we believe are the characteristics of a healthy society for the benefit of body, mind and spirit. That's what most of us are struggling with. But unless change is effected at a third and deepest level, the level of people's foundational **beliefs**, we won't see the profound change we all look for.

How do we achieve these levels of change? We could - we do - pray and we trust God for the future. But is there anything else we can do? We can help to change the character of the Christian community, the Church, so that the Church will be a more effective agent to change the world for the better. And how will the Church change? Not simply by top-down institutional initiatives, however well-intentioned, but by re-invigorating Christian disciples - that is, everyone who bears the name of Christ, lay and ordained, ourselves included. When a bishop ordains a minister he or she reminds the congregation that

> 'in baptism, the whole Church is summoned to witness to God's love and to work for the coming of his kingdom'.[4]

It is undoubtedly true that many people in our churches do not identify with the word 'disciple' because they associate the term only with the disciples called by Jesus in his three-year ministry, people (men and some women) who were special, called to a different kind of faith from that of Christians today. If the story of Jesus and his disciples was written and preserved simply as history, then Christian discipleship would have ended with the death of the Apostles. So we will take a look in each of the following chapters at some passages of the Scriptures that have influenced my thinking and may stimulate yours. These extracts are by no means intended to be exhaustive selections but merely offerings for further consideration. For those who are less familiar with the documents of the New Testament, some groundwork needs to be done to explore what these writings aimed to achieve.

One of the motives behind the writing of the first three Gospels was to get the story down while some of the main actors were still alive - one ancient tradition says that Mark wrote at the dictation of Peter - and the Fourth Gospel assumes we have read at least one of the others. But there had to be a second, more important, motive: to leave a story from which succeeding generations could learn. So, for instance, when Jesus was angry with the disciples for keeping the children away from him,[5] we are being prompted to ask ourselves whether what he taught and did on that occasion was for the benefit of the Twelve alone? Of course not! It was recorded for the benefit of the readers, and of readers in succeeding generations – for us. Take that to an extreme and we find some Christians wielding the Bible as if it were a lethal weapon, throwing it at their opponents (for so they must regard them). A far better approach is to invite people into the story, to become participants in the action, to listen as if we are the first hearers of the message. The biblical writers wanted us to put ourselves in their shoes, to step into the story. In what follows, it is only when we grasp this fundamental principle that we begin to see the connections between the call and challenge of the first disciples as described in the New Testament and our own call.

Some critics of a recent renewed emphasis on discipleship suggest that it is inward-looking, focussing attention on the membership of the Church rather than on its purpose; that it is sectarian vocabulary, dividing the Church from others and emphasizing a them-and-us mentality. With so many challenges facing humanity, the argument continues, any discussion of discipleship is a concentration on peripheral and esoteric church business. The argument, at its root, concerns the extent to which a disciple is committed not only to the love of God but also to the whole of God's creation. Put another way, a disciple of Christ is first of all a child of creation: the theology of discipleship begins with humanity created in God's image. Disciples in the New Testament are never described as being a group of people isolated from the world or as being inducted into a secret society. On the contrary, the call of Christ to fall-in behind him, to be willing to carry the cross for his sake and that of the world he loves, is a call to life in its fullness.

We need to define what we're talking about. In chapter 3 I will deal with the different uses of 'disciple', 'apostle', and other expressions that are readily confused with one another. For our present purposes 'disciple' means 'Christian'. It's time for a revival of discipleship.

Literally, disciples are 'people who put their mind to something', that is, they are learners. (The Latin word *'discipulus'* also means 'a learner'.) Disciples bound themselves to a *'didaskalos'*, a teacher. The word applied not only to academic study but also to apprenticeships, and involved a binding relationship between apprentice and master. Apprenticeships then and now are undertaken over a period of time and apprentices learn the language, values, responsibilities and conduct of their trade; they see the craft through the eyes of their mentors and become like them.

However, though apprentices progress to becoming craftspeople, there is no equivalent graduation from being a disciple.

The 1985 Church of England report entitled *'All Are Called'* included a Common Statement that sets out some important principles.

'Because all human beings are made in the image of God, they are called to become the People of God, the Church, servants and ministers and citizens of the Kingdom, a new humanity in Jesus Christ. Though we are tainted by our sinfulness, God's wonderful grace and love offer us all this common Christian vocation. God leaves everyone free to refuse this call; but the call is there for all without exception.

'The young are called; the elderly are called. There is no retirement from the Christian pilgrimage. ...

'God "has no favourites" ... There is no special status in the Kingdom ... Nor does our calling – our vocation – depend on any kind of ordination. There are still many deep controversies about what ordination may signify, in many Churches and within our own Church of England. But it certainly does not indicate any special 'grade' of Christian, more holy than the laity. And for everybody, bishops, priests and laity together, the great sacrament of our common calling is our baptism, which signifies our glorious new life in Christ.'[6]

Four years earlier, David Watson had written that

'Christians in the West have largely neglected what it means to be a disciple of Christ. The vast majority of western Christians are church-members, pew-fillers, hymn-singers, sermon-tasters, Bible-readers, even born-again-believers or Spirit-filled-charismatics - but not true disciples of Jesus. If we were willing to learn the meaning of real discipleship and actually to become disciples, the church in the West would be transformed, and the resultant impact on society would be staggering.'[7]

That leads us to ask how we could improve the way we make and sustain disciples in what is called 'the emerging culture' in which we all live, whatever our nation, and how the Church's public ministry can and should sustain disciples. What I propose here is to take a good look at a few biblical examples and extrapolate some principles from them. If you are looking for the latest fail-safe method for making disciples, a *'Teach yourself Making Disciples'*, then you've wasted your money on this book because I am no fan of whatever happens to be the latest method! After many years as a practitioner, I don't think there is a trick, any technique that can be applied successfully everywhere: we just have to get on with what God calls us to do – 'living as Christ himself lived'.[8] Making and sustaining disciples is about concentrating on people, so a start may be to spend a good deal less time in front of a laptop or tablet and, instead, to get among the people God loves and make Christ visible.

Heavenly Father,
you revealed your love
by sending your only Son into the world
that all might live through him:
grant that by the power of the Spirit
your Church may obey his command
to make disciples of all nations;
through Jesus Christ our Lord.
Amen.

(A collect for mission)

References

1. Richard V Pearce: Conflicting Understandings of Christian Conversion: A Missiological Challenge, in the International Bulletin of Missionary Research, January 2004 (vol 28, no 1)
2. The Death of Christian Britain, Routledge, 2001.
3. The Barna Group, Perceptions of Jesus: Christians & Evangelism in England 2015.
4. Common Worship Ordinal.
5. Mark 10. 13-16; and see Matthew 19. 13-15; Luke 18. 15-17.
6. All Are Called: Towards a Theology of the Laity.
7. David Watson: Discipleship, (1981).
8. 1 John 2. 6.

2 The Call

'When Christ calls a man, He bids him come and die.'

Such famous words from Dietrich Bonhoeffer who proved his willingness to lose his life in an attempt to defeat Nazism. He continued,

'It may be a death like that of the first disciples who had to leave home and work to follow Him, or it may be a death like Luther's, who had to leave the monastery and go out into the world. But it is the same death every time - death in Jesus Christ, the death of the old man at His call. That is why the rich young man was so loath to follow Jesus, for the cost of following was the death of his will. In fact every command of Jesus is a call to die, with all our affections and lusts. But we do not want to die, and therefore Jesus Christ and His call are necessarily our death and our life.'[1]

The call of God is a first step on the Christian disciple's journey. That first call may have been in baptism, though increasingly these days baptism follows the response to God's first knock on the door. Sensing God's call can be difficult when the background noise in a secular, consumerist society - and particularly in parts of the educational system - blares out, 'No one believes that religious stuff any more!' Background noise can take many forms, but, if a person can for a moment identify and turn down the volume of secular spin, the voice of God can still be heard, and is heard today.

'Only when I kill all noise
do I hear that still small voice.'[2]

Let's take a look at the call of Moses as a useful place to begin in thinking about the nature of God's call, 'Come!'

'The angel of the Lord appeared to Moses in a flame of fire out of a bush. He looked, and the bush was blazing, yet it was not consumed. Then Moses said, "I must turn aside and look at this great sight, and see why the bush is not burned up." When the LORD saw that Moses had turned aside to see, God called to him out of the bush, "Moses, Moses!" and he said, "Here I am." Then he said, "Come no closer! Remove the sandals from your feet, for the place on which you are standing is holy ground." He said further, "I am the God of your father the God of Abraham, the God of Isaac and the God of Jacob." And Moses hid his face, for he was afraid to look at God ...'

'God said, "So come, I will send you to Pharaoh, to bring my people, the Israelites, out of Egypt".'[3]

Moses, a shepherd, a fugitive from justice, a wanderer, is confronted by 'the angel of the Lord', which, at this stage in the biblical story, is a neat way of describing God in human terms - in a living bush which is on fire but is not burnt up. Confused? So was Moses.

Quite likely, what this story means to you is conditioned by the way you first heard it; for those who are older, perhaps it was the subject of one of your first religious drawings as a child. And that's the way the story works. We can say that the fire represents purity, holiness or the flames of God's presence leaping from earth to heaven. For the reader of the Hebrew Scriptures, the fire itself is the glory of the Lord. Incongruously this fire of God's glory is seen to be burning within a living plant, something that the desert-dweller would associate with an oasis and life: God's glory burns inside life - it begins to remind us of the life of God in human flesh - but that's a later story.

For a reader familiar with the New Testament the fire will also evoke the image of the Holy Spirit descending on the apostles on the Day of Pentecost.[4] While it would be anachronistic to read Pentecost into the story of the burning bush, there is much that the burning bush can tell us about the power of holiness, a primary gift of the Holy Spirit.

What starts as Moses' apparently mundane curiosity – 'I will go closer and see this' - seems to provoke God into taking the initiative and calling Moses by name. Of course, when we refer to God 'calling us by name', few of us would be able to say that we have ever identified a voice because the call of God is usually voiceless. We talk about 'calling' because so many of the characters in the Bible and in other stories of the saints are presented as hearing a voice or seeing a vision or dreaming. Without suggesting for a moment that it can't or doesn't happen that way sometimes, experience tells us that God's more familiar mode of calling is by leading us into situations and events that we recognise as his 'call' much later after the event. In the strange way that faith has, we understand when the bishop says in confirmation, 'God has called you by name and made you his own.' It is the Spirit who calls and makes us the daughters, sons and heirs of God.

Moses is told to come no closer and to remove his sandals; he hides his face in awe and fear of looking at God himself. God is not an object in the world: we'd be closer to the mark to say that the world is in God. Even asking the question about whether God exists is almost to classify him with other things, which is exactly what you can't do with God. He is never One among many, nor an object of human knowledge. It is only because of God that we can know anything at all. The Lord revealed to Moses, we read, is no new God but the One who had been worshipped by the ancestors of Moses' people - his own father, Abraham, Isaac and Jacob - the God of whom he would have heard from the Hebrews enslaved in Egypt. Despite reciting this fine religious pedigree, the story gives us the impression that, at this stage, Moses was a very unlikely candidate for a religious leader, having been brought up in the Egyptian royal house, anything but a devout environment! God does not do stereo-typing and often chooses the unlikely candidates and fails to choose the obvious ones or sometimes calls the likely people to the most unlikely tasks. Moses is one of innumerable people on the edge who are called by God to do his work.

For instance, more than 1,000 years before the birth of Christ Samuel was destined to be a priest, called as a prophet and was to become the last and greatest judge of Israel. As a child, he hears the call of the Lord with such reality that he thinks someone else is calling him from down the corridor. It's another intriguing story[5] that can lose some of its force by familiarity. The clarity of the call is more obvious because Samuel is portrayed as a very young child who is not carrying any religious baggage. The Lord goes on to tell the boy that he must speak a word of judgement to the prevailing religious establishment, including his superior and mentor, so the account is full of the anxiety that a child would feel in carrying such a burden. This crisis in the child's mind[6] highlights the difference between conversion, the first step, giving one's life to the Lord, and discipleship, the long-term consequences of a life lived for him.

The prophet Isaiah's calling is a classic in many ways, located at a specific moment in history, the unhappy end of a long reign in 742 BC.[7] The call comes in another impressionist vision filled with images of purification, holiness and worship, and culminates in the Lord issuing a challenge: 'Whom shall I send? Who will go for us?' From the days when the Bible was read every day in school assemblies, ex-pupils may recall the answer: 'Here am I. Send me!' Stirring stuff that challenges all who hear it to willing, selfless service. (The idea in school was to inculcate in the pupils those traditional values of service, stiff upper lip, and so on.) Yet rarely did anyone read on to the Lord's job description for the prophet:

'Go, tell this people, "However hard you listen, you will never understand. However hard you look, you will never perceive." This people's wits are dulled; they have stopped their ears and shut their eyes, so that they may not see with their eyes, nor listen with their ears, nor understand with their wits, and then turn and be healed.'[8]

It turns out that Isaiah's is a calling to proclaim judgement and includes a built-in prediction of failure. It's all very well to say, 'Send me!' but what if being sent will turn out to be a personal disaster? We are reminded of the words of Jesus,

'No one is worthy of me who does not take up his cross and follow me. Whoever gains his life will lose it; whoever loses his life for my sake will gain it.'[9]

In or about 626 BC Jeremiah was a young man when he was called to a prophetic ministry; he protested, 'I am not skilled in speaking; I am too young.' So he was given a vision of the Lord touching his mouth to bestow the gift of speech and authority. His ministry to proclaim exile and the shutting-down of the institutions of religious life was summed-up in his job description 'to uproot and to pull down, to destroy and to demolish', as was the message of ultimate hope and promise, 'to build and to plant',[10] both of which were acted out in the ensuing story. Jeremiah was no 'joiner', yet such was the burden of his calling and the resultant persecution that at times he was prone to despair and to taking it out on the Lord.[11] John Milton (1708-74) was another Jeremiah who exemplified this granite-hard, holy, child-like faith:

'I cannot praise a fugitive and cloistered virtue, unexercised and unbreathed, that never sallies out and seeks her adversary, but slinks out of the race, where that immortal garland is to be run for, not without dust and heat. Assuredly we bring not innocence into the world, we bring impurity much rather: that which purifies us is trial, and trial is by what is contrary.'[12]

In the New Testament, Saul of Tarsus, a deeply orthodox Hebrew,[13] was arrested by the risen Christ at a high point in his passionate persecution of Christians, and called to bring the good news to gentiles. That conversion on the road to Damascus, [14] to which the apostle refers to in his correspondence and repeatedly returns in what we read of his witness in Acts,[15] was a spiritual turn-around of his life from which there could be no return. Paul defended his apostleship and his mission to take the gospel to the heathen world by tracing them both back to the Damascus road calling.

That's to say nothing of post-biblical characters like Augustine the African (354-430), who had an illegitimate son at 18 years old, toyed with a variety of religious and philosophical systems of belief, became a sceptic and is reputed to have prayed, 'Give me chastity and continence, but not yet!' As he began to turn to the Faith, he recalled the words, 'How long, O Lord? Will you be angry for ever?' and heard the voice of a child chanting, 'Tolle, lege!' ['Pick up and read!'] which led him to return to Paul's Letter to the Romans, that he had just put down. Doing so, he recalled,

'I seized, opened, and in silence read the passage upon which my eyes first fell: "Not in revelry and drunkenness, not in immorality or indecency, not in fighting or jealousy, but put on the Lord Jesus Christ and stop paying attention to your sinful nature and satisfying its desires." No further would I read, nor was there any need for, instantly, at the end of this sentence, as though my heart was flooded with a light of peace, all the shadows of doubt melted away."[16]

Augustine was to become one of the greatest of the post-biblical theologians in the Church.

Francis of Assisi (1181/2-1226) was born into the family of a prosperous silk merchant and lived life in the fast lane as a soldier. On his way to war, Francis had a vision calling him back to Assisi where he rejected his inherited wealth. Subsequently, making a pilgrimage to Rome, he joined some beggars and the experience moved him to live in poverty. Returning home he began preaching in the streets, and formed an order for men which was also an inspiration for the founding of an order for women. He was never ordained to the priesthood but the call of God to the poor transformed his life and has transformed many since. The Franciscan movement broke fresh ground in terms of the religious life in that it took as its model the community of Jesus' disciples, always on the move, preaching the gospel of repentance, forgiveness and transformation, travelling light, as contrasted with the early Church pattern of stable, gathered communities in one place that had been the model for, say, the Benedictines. Whether gathered or itinerant, the monastic movements were mediaeval re-discoveries of discipleship.

Within our own culture, C.S. Lewis (who was later to become a professor of Anglo-Saxon literature) had a blandly Christian childhood but embraced rationalist atheism as a teenager. In 1929, the God he 'so earnestly desired not to meet' came to him.[17]

'I was going up Headington Hill on the top of a bus. Without words and almost without images, a fact about myself was somehow presented to me. I became aware that I was holding something at bay, or shutting something out.'

Alone in his room in Magdalen College, Oxford, one night, he recounted,

'I gave in, and admitted that God was God, and knelt and prayed: perhaps that night, the most dejected and reluctant convert in all England'.

Two years later he made a specific commitment to faith in Christ:

'I was driven to Whipsnade one sunny morning. When we set out I did not believe that Jesus Christ is the Son of God and when we reached the zoo I did.'

He reflected that this was not a 'search for God' but the 'compelling embrace' of joy.

In 2018, Clare, a teacher in a Yorkshire primary school, wandered away from God until the influence of Christian friends brought her back to taking the good news seriously so that, over a period of 15 years, Christ came to the centre of her life. Hers is a non-untypical testimony to God's call over a period of time.

In each case the circumstances mattered: none of the saints of God are called out of the blue. The context in which God calls and the person senses it – on the run, in the desert, in a dormitory, during worship, as a youth, as a soldier, on a journey, in a study, among beggars or on a bus - is part of the call. Increasingly, faith is not the default position in western society. It has been well said that,

'Christianity is no longer a faith one opts out of but a faith which one has to opt for. One no longer has to have a reason for not practising Christianity, but a reason for starting, or, for those with a Christian upbringing, a reason for continuing.'[18]

So when we speak about God 'calling' it may or may not mean a voice that is heard, but certainly we sense the Spirit leading us on from where we are to where he wants us to be; and not only with our five physical senses but with fear, love and a range of other emotions. Hearing and responding to the call of God is as simple and natural as breathing. There are, nevertheless, times when we need to be sure that what we hear is not our own desire but the voice of the living God. The Bible relates many stories of God calling through the internal workings of the mind – just think of how important dreams are to the callings of the Old Testament Patriarchs Jacob and Joseph, to Mary and Joseph in the Gospel and to Peter on the Day of Pentecost[19] – but in each case, it is God himself, not an inner voice, who speaks. In an age when interest in spirituality disconnected from faith is increasing, it is not unlikely that any talk of 'calling' will be misinterpreted as describing a message from one's own inner being – a voice from within. Christians (and other people of faith) have always affirmed that a true call comes from God, from outside one's own being, however it is expressed.

It is easier to discern what God is saying now when we appreciate the ways in which he has called his people in the past; in other words, as we become familiar with the over-arching message of the Scriptures. Reading the Bible in the community of faith with a grateful and critical sense of the past, a vigorous engagement with where, when and who we are, and with patient hope for the future we can begin to discern the voice of God from other sounds.

When calling is too convenient it can possibly signify a problem. One suspects that some of the mass baptisms in these islands in pagan times might have been for mixed motives. The danger is ever present. Making the decision to follow Christ because it seems to work is no substitute for using our minds to work out whether it seems to be true. It is crucially important for authentic evangelism that people should be called to discipleship with integrity, because there is no more important a decision to be made than the one to respond to the call of God in Christ. Archbishop Thomas Becket, in T.S Eliot's play 'Murder in the Cathedral' memorably struggles with his integrity in the face of martyrdom:

'The last temptation is the greatest treason:
To do the right deed for the wrong reason.'[23]

Again and again the Gospel of John explores what we might call the evidence on which faith rests, pointing us to Jesus himself as the object of faith.[20] Periodically, he even reports Jesus' frustration that people keep looking for signs: 'Will none of you ever believe without seeing signs and portents?'[21] As the crisis in the Gospel intensifies over who Jesus is, he points to the contrast between the material evidence, the signs, and faith in him. To the question, 'Are you the Messiah?' Jesus replies,

'I have told you, and you do not believe. My deeds done in my Father's name are my credentials, but because you are not sheep of my flock you do not believe. My own sheep listen to my voice; I know them and they follow me.'[22]

The people see the deeds but they don't have the trusting relationship that enables them to hear and follow the Shepherd's voice.

When people speak of 'vocation' they frequently mean a calling to the public ministry of the Church, and often specifically to ordination. Unfortunately, churches have colluded in this. It is important to underline that the word 'vocation' simply means 'calling', God's call of a person to discipleship or the call of a disciple to a particular activity. Vocation to public ministry is but one of the innumerable callings for a Christian disciple and it's about time we stopped hi-jacking that word.

If God is calling someone to a caring role, he normally uses carers; for evangelism, he may use evangelists; for teaching, teachers; for woodwork, carpenters; and so on.

So, for any work in relation to church he involves the church and we should rightly expect the church (in its local expression and more widely) to be involved both in the call itself and in the testing of the call.

Sven Erik-Brodd has commented on developments in our understanding of calling within the second half of the twentieth century - in this case he was writing of vocation to ordained ministry but it applies generally.

> 'The idea of vocation had changed from the Church's calling of a person ... to the idea of a particular person's identification of a calling for themselves, which should be accepted by the Church. This idea of calling or vocation was formed by Pietism, a movement contemporary and sometimes intertwined with Enlightenment.'[24]

It's a warning against the privatisation of God's call, of talk about 'my vocation'. Bells ring in my head when someone comes to me with a clearly-defined and neatly-packaged call, conveniently fitted into their personal circumstances. It is our duty in God's name to ask serious questions of such a sense of calling in order to discern whether it is indeed a response to the voice of God or merely a noble aspiration. God calls *in* a context, *from* a context, *to* a context – and it's often inconvenient. Calling is rooted in our own context but it may uproot us to another.

Vocation doesn't happen just once in a lifetime because we keep finding ourselves called in one way or another; and it is particular to you and to me - what earlier generations used to call 'peculiar', meaning 'my own personally' - a call unique to each individual and situation.

The most important things in life, like being born or dying or being baptized, happen to you: you're 'passive', as they say, not in control. Being called by God is like that. You and other people can create conditions favourable to calling but God alone calls. Our part is to respond to the call, to tune in to God's will, to trust and to obey, to fall-in - none of the words we can use does justice to the variety and significance of our human response.

> 'It is in the nature of humanity to be called by God, regardless of age, personality, energy, intellect, sex, influence, employment, or any other characteristic or definition ...
> 'car dealers and cleaners are called just as much as professors and lawyers and missionary nurses.'[25]

Being alert to the circumstances of God's call should make us aware of the part other people play in speaking and acting as God's messengers. My own call to ordained ministry intrigues me even today. From as young as I can remember, my father (a Scottish Presbyterian) told me that he prayed daily for me to be called to ministry. It takes little imagination to guess the reaction of a normal, rebellious youth: I wanted to be a criminal lawyer. Having come to faith in my teens, I saw no reason to change what I believed was my future career. Until one day, when a friend of the family who was a sympathetic but non-church agnostic said, over a cup of tea, 'Why do you want to be a lawyer? You should be in the Church!' That was the first time ministry had seriously occurred to me; I blurted out some foolish reply but it set something going that, in time, led to my asking the local vicar if I could see him. I told him the story and to my surprise he replied that he and others were expecting this but had decided to wait until it had occurred to me! It was far more difficult to eat humble pie and tell my father. 'I knew God would hear my prayer,' he replied with a wry smile, 'though I can't understand why he should choose the Church of England!' God calls through circumstances and often uses the most unlikely messengers.

In my experience there is some truth in the reflection of James Francis, that

'Vocation begins with where we are, but it is really all about the summons to go in search of ourselves in responding to God's call through Christ.'[26]

Those who recognise and act on the call of God discover something important about themselves in the process. It seems to me that the servants of God have all uncovered truths about themselves in his call.

Unlike the things we buy in shops there's no 'best before' date on the call of God. Early in my ministry I worked in a diocese that consisted of a busy urban area where we young ministers thought all the parishes were 'challenging' and a large rural area where we thought all the parishes were 'sleepy'. So, when one of our number was asked to go to one of the rural parishes, he asked the bishop how long he'd have to stay there. The bishop's reply was simple: 'You're called to minister there until and unless God and the Church call you elsewhere.' That's not a bad working principle. God's call takes you on your pilgrimage one step at a time and there's nowhere to opt-out for a while; the only destination we can be certain of is 'the city that is to come'.[27]

Back to Moses. This unlikely person - a poor speaker, a murderer-on-the-run, an alien from a people in captivity: he was to go back to the King of Egypt, someone he might have feared most, and bring the Israelites out of slavery, leaving the Egyptians with a seriously depleted construction workforce. An unlikely mission to the ruler of a nation that had expelled its old ruling dynasty, was enlarging its empire, building new cities and growing in international status. Moses had already shown himself to be a natural coward: God has some funny ideas when it comes to choosing his agents.

So what resources was Moses offered? A stick, a colleague (Aaron) and a new, personal name for God: YHWH (Yahweh), the LORD[28] - a word impossible to translate because it can mean so much: 'I live', 'I am the One and Only', 'I alone exist in my own right', 'I am the One who is and who will be', 'I am who I am', 'He who is'. It's a name that attempts to describe the God who is so unique there's no collective noun that includes him; you can't add up God and anything else, even the universe, and make two. All that we value will change, decay and die, nothing is for ever - except God. Everything is dependent, created - except God. Unique, yet in a sense personal: he has a name.

Some people have a name for everything in the house: the car (Jezebel because she's unfaithful), the pet rabbit (Fierce Bad Rabbit), the bicycle (Charity because the tyres are 'not puffed up'), the toaster (Alfred, who burned the cakes), and so on. To name an object is to say something about its character or, in the case of a child, to express one's hopes for the child's future. But no one has the right to name God. God's personal name, by which he was to be addressed only in worship, is a revealed name. And the greatest revealed name of all is even more intimate than 'Yahweh': it is 'Abba', the first gurglings of a baby, the natural name for the adopted sons and daughters of God to use of their heavenly Father.[29]

> 'This is but a little word,' wrote Martin Luther, 'and yet it comprehends everything. The mouth does not speak, but the feelings of the heart are spoken in this way. Even if I am oppressed with anguish and terror on every side and seem to have been forsaken and utterly cast away from your presence, yet I am your child and you are my Father for Christ's sake: I am loved because of the Beloved. Therefore this little word, "Abba Father", conceived effectively in the heart, passes all the eloquence of Demosthenes, Cicero, and of the most eloquent rhetoricians that ever were in the world. For here, the feelings of the heart are expressed with sighs which cannot be expressed by tongue or words of eloquence.'[30]

It's worth observing that 'Abba' is not a sexist male word. When a child makes a sound that its parents hear as a first word, there's normally some friendly rivalry over whether it's 'Mamma' or 'Dadda'; the reality is that it's neither, but an early sign of recognition and communication - the 'Abba' moment.

Moses, the unlikely one, was called by God - a proto-disciple. Jesus calls today. He calls you and me. God calls people in as many ways as there are people. The primary call is the call of the Father, the Son and the Spirit inherent in our baptism. Archbishop Rowan Williams wisely mused,

'Perhaps baptism really ought to have some health warnings attached to it: "If you take this step, if you go into these depths, it will be transfiguring, exhilarating, life-giving and very, very dangerous." To be baptized into Jesus is not to be in what the world thinks of as a safe place. Jesus' first disciples discovered that in the Gospels, and his disciples have gone on discovering it ever since.'[31]

The call of Christ is ultimately a call to sacrifice.

To Moses, the first word is, 'Come closer!' - the call from God who, in the words of the Apostle Paul, 'called you to have fellowship with his Son Jesus Christ our Lord'. [32] We begin with God calling us into communion with Christ and his people. Herein lies the danger of becoming inward-looking, becoming so obsessed with conversion, the inner life and belonging to the Church, that we don't ask ourselves why God wants us in his team.

The instruction that immediately followed the call of Moses was 'Go!' that is, to be God's agent in rescuing his people from slavery. The call of Jesus to be his disciples is a call to pray for and live the kingdom of God, the realm of God's activity. Disciples of Christ are not simply students of theology but those who learn from Jesus in his day-by-day encounters with the world. The call to be a disciple is a call to reject the kind of power known to politicians and secular leadership programmes, and to accept the power of the Holy Spirit.

One of the few downsides of the charismatic renewal movements of the last half century has been loose talk about 'power' that so very easily prompts the question, 'What's in it for me?' Any answer, however piously expressed, that suggests God's power is a personal possession or some kind of 'perk' of discipleship is a heinous denial of grace. The resources of God's power, the power of the Spirit 'at work among us',[33] define the meaning of discipleship: the glory of God and the work of his kingdom.

This contrast between secular power and the hidden power of childlike simplicity is a theme Mark plays with in the middle chapters of his Gospel. The disciples James and John had confused these concepts of power by asking for special places in the kingdom of God.[34] John N. Collins comments on the ensuing conversation between

Jesus and the disciples:

'Jesus's opening comment – "this is not your way" – brusquely disillusions anyone living in hope of honour. A new kind of society opens before those who have been harbouring visions of a share in imperial greatness. In terms of social reward and personal satisfaction, the panorama is bleak. It is empty of the timeless symbols of upward mobility, dignity and success. The contrast between the political and social realities of the first century and the conditions of being within a discipleship of the Son of Man is absolute. So absolute in fact that there is no point of contact between them. ... Within the realm of discipleship operate forces unknown to emperors and military champions. ... Jesus insists that discipleship does not operate by the principles that make one "great" or "first". Instead, discipleship operates by principles that no social organization has ever known; rather, the sayings propose that discipleship is not a sociological function at all. The contrast with empire indicates that discipleship functions at a level where power does not exist. The situation is not only that power is inappropriate within discipleships, but that discipleship is an environment which is not receptive of power.'[35]

All who are involved in church leadership, like me, need to take these words to heart in our exercise of the powers conferred on us by our office.

Christian disciples are people called to be empowered not by self or status but by the Spirit, to be permanently engaged in God's action, people whose growing communion with him affirms the hope to which all are called:

'I pray that the God of our Lord Jesus Christ, the all-glorious Father, may confer on you the spiritual gifts of wisdom and vision, with the knowledge of him that they bring. I pray that your inward eyes may be enlightened, so that you may know what is the hope to which he calls you, how rich and glorious is the share he offers you among his people in their inheritance, and how vast are the resources of his power open to us who have faith.'[36]

Almighty God,
by whose grace alone we are accepted and called to your service:
strengthen us by your Holy Spirit
and make us worthy of our calling;
through Jesus Christ your Son our Lord.
Amen.

(Collect of the 5th Sunday before Lent)

References

1. The Cost of Discipleship, 1937.
2. Harry Baker: But in silence.
3. Exodus 3. 2-6, 10.
4. Acts 2.
5. 1 Samuel 3.
6. Verses 10-18.
7. Isaiah 6. 1-10.
8. ibid.
9. Matthew 10. 38.
10. Jeremiah 1. 4-10.
11. Jeremiah 20. 7.
12. Areopagitica.
13. See Philippians 3. 4-9
14. Acts 9. 1-30.
15. Acts 22 and 26.
16. Confessions, Book VIII, (c. 400). The date was about AD 386 and the passage was Romans 13. 13b-14.
17. Surprised by Joy, 1955.
18. Christopher Harris & Richard Startup: The Church in Wales, The Sociology of a Traditional Institution, University of Wales Press, 1999.
19. See Genesis chapters 28, 31, 32, 37, 40-42; Matthew chapters 1, 2; Joel 2. 28; Acts 2. 17.
20. See John 2. 31, etc.
21. John 4. 48.
22. John 10. 25-27.
23. Part I, lines 667-8.
24. The diaconate as ecumenical opportunity, International Journal for the Study of the Christian Church (13.4), 2014.
25. All are Called: Towards a Theology of the Laity - Church of England report, 1985.
26. Discipleship and Vocation, in 'Rural Theology' Issue 73, 2009.
27. Hebrews 11. 16; 13. 14.
28. When this word is intended in the Old Testament of English bibles it is frequently printed in capital letters.
29. Galatians 4. 6.
30. Commenting on Galatians 4. 6.
31. Being Christian, SPCK, 2014, p 9.
32. 1 Corinthians 1. 9.
33. Ephesians 3. 16, 20.

34. Mark 10. 35-45.
35. Diakonia in the Teaching of Jesus, in Diakonia Studies, Oxford, 2014, pp 85-6.
36. Ephesians 1. 17, 18.

3 Called to be Disciples

Let's look at the specifics of calling, the call to be a disciple of Jesus Christ. At times of crisis in the Church's life - and this is such a time for the Church in Europe and elsewhere - the challenge is to nurture disciples, not simply to make converts. To repeat: disciples are converts but not all converts are disciples. Converts are those who have been changed; disciples change the world.

Dallas Willard described the issue of poor or non-existent discipleship as

'the elephant in the Western Church. It's there in the middle of all we do. We walk around it, make allowances for it and try to live with it. But we rarely name it as the biggest obstacle in our missional task, and are even less likely to intentionally try to shift it. The plain fact is that the Church in England and Wales is lacking in discipleship. We have much to learn from Christians in other parts of the world.'[1]

You may ask, as many have done, why some people who are searching for meaning, purpose and hope in life and seeking out spiritual answers - often looking at Jesus Christ among others - are not looking to the Church for help. Ask them why not and you are likely to get answers such as these, particularly from younger people:
· Eh? What's Church got to do with anything?
· I don't believe in fairy tales.
· Why should I? The Church says 'No!' to everything.
· The Church has forgotten God.
· The Church hates science because science has disproved religion.
· I have nothing in common with the Church.
· The Church is full of small-minded hypocrites.

Whether people are right or wrong, they certainly make remarks like this - I overheard the last one from someone using their mobile phone in a supermarket. How do we respond?

We could get some expert apologist for the Christian way to appear on prime-time television and explain it all so lucidly that critics will realise the folly of their thinking and everyone will understand the gospel and appreciate the Church. Look out of the window and you may see some pigs flying past at the same time. You might invite the woman in the supermarket to an evangelistic event or to a supper that will lead into an introductory course on the Christian faith; great for a few but not for many. You could invite someone to a church service but, let's be honest, in some places that might not be the most attractive prospect.

Then there's the curious way employed by some people of communicating the good news by simply speaking louder - and shouting if they think no one is listening! This technique reminds me of conversations between my late mother in her 80's and a French lady of a similar age: neither spoke the other's language but reasoned that speaking louder and slower would overcome the problem. One being a Celt and the other Gallic, though the languages didn't get through to either party, the gestures did. Shouting the gospel ever louder using a vocabulary that the other party can't understand simply produces more heat than light; it's the gestures, the actions of a redeemed life, that may get through. I am convinced that we will not communicate the joy and fulfilment of being a Christian and belonging to the Church simply by turning up the volume. A church which shouts loudly but whose message is hollow won't be heard. A church whose members are mean-spirited will be pitied. A church that is preoccupied with its own survival will rightly be ignored.

So what will get through? Counter-intuitive though it may appear to some, if Christians are to communicate the gospel effectively, our words will have to be sparing and follow, rather than precede, our actions. People need to notice that something is different, holy, consecrated, and they will see that when it is embodied in disciples. Then they may ask why.

Mark's Gospel describes the scenes when Jesus called his first disciples. In both of these extracts from the early chapters of Mark's Gospel, Jesus is at the lakeside where so much of significance happens.

'Jesus was walking by the sea of Galilee when he saw Simon and his brother Andrew at work with casting-nets in the lake; for they were fishermen. Jesus said to them, "Come, follow me, and I will make you fishers of men." At once they left their nets and followed him.' ...

'Once more he went out to the lakeside. All the crowd came to him there, and he taught them. As he went along, he saw Levi son of Alphaeus at his seat in the custom-house, and said to him, "Follow me"; and he rose and followed him. When Jesus was having a meal in his house, many tax-collectors and sinners were seated with him and his disciples, for there were many of them among his followers. Some scribes who were Pharisees, observing the company in which he was eating, said to his disciples, "Why does he eat with tax-collectors and sinners?" Hearing this, Jesus said to them, "It is not the healthy who need a doctor, but the sick; I did not come to call the virtuous, but sinners." '[2]

Simon and Andrew were certainly not among the landless poor – we know that Zebedee, their father, had hired servants. To these middle-class entrepreneurial fishermen Mark tells us that Jesus gave a curt military order - an order which the two apparently could not refuse: 'Come after me!' They were not becoming disciples of yet another rabbi because, although Jesus will spend some time and energy teaching them over the next three years, the purpose of his calling is to invite them to share an apostolic task, that of proclaiming the Kingdom of God. 'I will make you fish for people' might have had unpleasant overtones for Simon and Andrew, if they remembered Jeremiah describing the Lord 'fishing' for evil people and hunting them down! But these new disciples are being called by Jesus to fish for people in order to save them, to heal them, to make them whole. They were called to a mission of repentance and faith in community.[3] Once the band of disciples had been formed around Simon, Andrew, James and John, the four fishermen, Jesus' ministry began to take shape and started to make sense.

When the leadership of the Church of England decided that it was time for a focus on discipleship, rather than ministry, finance or any other supporting concern, Linda Woodhead wrote in *The Church Times* that discipleship was a 'theologically peripheral concept', and Canon Angela Tilby cheekily followed this up by referring to 'the d-word', dismissing it as 'sectarian vocabulary' derived from American evangelicalism. I know what they are saying, that being Christian is not just about getting people to join the Church but also about involvement in local communities and the transformation of God's world in peace and justice. Yes, there is always the danger of being harnessed to a particular view of truth, particularly one that suits another culture, yet how any plain reading of these crucial Gospel stories could dismiss discipleship as 'peripheral' or 'sectarian' beats me.

The Revised English Bible used above dares to use the word 'men' because there is a deliberate emphasis, not on the sex of the disciples or their converts but on the fulfilment of their occupation. They are 'fishers' (*halieis* in Greek) and are to find fulfilment as 'men-fishers' (*halieis anthropon*); at the command of Jesus they leave behind what they are and begin a new life towards what they will be. They are learners and have commenced a journey towards their fulfilment as apostles. Roger Walton[4] stresses that disciples are formed through worship, community and mission - in being *with* Jesus and his community, *for* the wider community, *in* God's mission.

What that means for the Church is that the whole community of faith is called to the discipleship of God's mission: we are, each and all, missionary disciples and the Church herself is mission-shaped. Don't let's make an enormous leap in our thinking to assume that, because we are all equally members of the community of missionary disciples, we all have to exercise some ministry in that community. No, it's simply that we are all responsible for being missionary in our discipleship, including those of us in leadership who can sometimes become so involved in maintaining the institution that we ignore this primary calling.

Pope Francis has written:

'The new evangelization calls for personal involvement on the part of each of the baptized. Every Christian is challenged, here and now, to be actively engaged in evangelization; indeed, anyone who has truly experienced God's saving love does not need much time or lengthy training to go out and proclaim that love. Every Christian is a missionary to the extent that he or she has encountered the love of God in Christ Jesus: we no longer say that we are "disciples" and "missionaries", but rather that we are always "missionary disciples".'[5]

It is interesting to contrast the discipleship to which Jesus called his first apprentices - the curt order, 'Follow me!' - with the discipleship to which people were called by the Apostle Paul. Those converted through Paul's ministry were generally expected to exercise their discipleship in the place where they found themselves when they were called:

'Each one should accept the lot which the Lord has assigned him and continue as he was when God called him. That is the rule I give in all the churches.'[6]

This distinction between the more radical, apostolic calling of Jesus' first disciples and a more locally-rooted calling by Paul highlights something of the apostolic nature of leadership in the Church, that it is expected to be focussed on proclaiming the reign of God. In other words, the same call to discipleship leads some to a life of witness ('Christ in you'[7]) and some in addition to a ministry of proclamation. It has often been falsely assumed that, because the twelve disciples were called to exercise this ministry of proclamation - as in their being sent out two-by-two to drive out demons, heal the sick and proclaim the kingdom of God[8] - that it is a commission for all disciples. To claim that kind of apostolic ministry for all disciples is a distortion of what the New Testament as a whole means by being Christian.

Dietrich Bonhoeffer and many other scholars have puzzled over the difference between the language of discipleship in the four Gospels and the Acts of the Apostles and its absence from the rest of the New Testament: the word for 'disciple' (*mathêtes* in Greek) appears 264 times in the Gospels and Acts but nowhere else. The very earliest date for Mark's Gospel, generally considered the first to be written, is at the end of Paul's life. So we know that the letters Paul composed were completed before the Gospels and Acts. It's possible that he used 'apostle' to describe the Twelve and their companions because that's how he knew them, and preferred terms like 'saints', 'brothers and sisters', 'believers', etc. to describe Christians.[9] Writing as he was for audiences in the pagan world of the Roman Empire, Paul translated the teaching of Jesus about discipleship into teaching about faith and baptism. The other New Testament Letters and the Revelation come from later decades of the first century; why the word 'disciple' doesn't appear in them is not known. In Acts, the Twelve are called 'apostles', and others are called 'believers', 'disciples', 'followers of the Way' and 'Christians'.[10]

We might then ask why the Gospel writers do use the word. First, they used 'disciples' for the companions of John the Baptist and Jesus; by the end of the Gospels, they present these disciples as the model for all subsequent Christian discipleship.[11] Second, we know that the early Church had to deal with some lax behaviour in the new churches, so it is not unlikely that the emphasis in the Gospels on life in community and on the risks to life and limb, was a salutary warning to second and third generation Christians who might have been slipping back into a comfortable faith. Third, since the Gospels were motivated by a desire to get back to the origins of Christian faith, as Luke and John make explicit,[12] their emphasis on discipleship is likely to have been a deliberate reminder of the cost of faith in a secular world: simply being baptized and saying the right things – joining the club - might be a cop-out. Both Paul's emphasis on active faith and the Gospels' on the cost of discipleship teach us to take Christ seriously.

It would seem that over time Christians increasingly used the collective noun that can be translated as 'church' (with the sense of 'belonging to the Lord') and 'congregation' ('people called out'), rather than 'disciples'.

Every Christian disciple is called to be a witness who tells, using actions and words, what God has done in his or her life. That calling is neither conditional nor provisional; there are no exceptions. The good thing about being a witness is that you don't need to be an expert in anything since all you are called to do is recount your own experience of an event. Ancient history has always depended on the accounts of reliable eye-witnesses and, for that reason, witnesses were named wherever possible so that their testimony could be checked. (In fact, it's worth noting in passing that the documents of the New Testament vastly exceed, both in number and proximity to what they describe, any other literature from the ancient world, and the primary basis of their authority is reliable witness.) Thus, there are many references, not only in the Gospels but also elsewhere in the New Testament, to individuals and groups to whom reference could be made. Besides, if the person referred to was a well-known figure, a useful example might be drawn: for example, Peter's loss of faith in the storm[13] or his denial and rehabilitation[14] would be an inspiration to successive generations of Christians that Jesus does not give up on failures.

Witnesses in a court of law will be called to order if they presume to comment on matters of law, to apportion guilt, or to pronounce any kind of judgement. The job of witnesses in the legal system is to relate their experiences, to make a public declaration to the court of what they have seen and heard: we speak of someone 'testifying'. That word in the Greek of the New Testament is the same one from which we derive the word 'martyrdom'; it is no wonder that it came to be used of those who are willing to lose their lives for Christ, 'martyrs' or witnesses right up to death. Lifelong testimony is an indelible mark of the disciple. Living out Christ's call to 'Follow me!' is all it takes.

Bishop John V. Taylor told the story of an Indian catechist at the end of the nineteenth century who was dismissed from the church for some misdemeanour. Burdened with shame, knowing he would never again dare to preach, the man left the area and went to some far-off village where there was no Christian community at all. There, where he was completely unknown, where malicious gossip could never reach him, he settled down and made his living as a potter. The church never heard of him again and he died there. Years later it was decided to send a team of evangelists to that very place. They rented a house and began to tell the stories of Jesus. They were amazed when the crowd of villagers responded eagerly, 'We know the man you are talking about! He lived here for years!' 'No,' said the preachers, 'you don't understand. We are talking about Jesus Christ.' 'Well,' answered the people, 'he never told us his name. But the man you describe is our potter without a doubt.'[15]

That same bishop described mission as 'making Christ visible' and we adapted it as the strap-line of my former diocese: 'Together making Christ visible'. Ray Anderson makes the point that

'Where Christ is not clearly visible as the life of the community of faith, the boundary lines tend to become more visible, often to the exclusion of those who are themselves ambiguous with regard to their spiritual identity.'[16]

If disciples – of whom a small minority are also pastors - are failing to make Christ visible, being Christian, living Christianly, then the way into the community of faith becomes harder for those who might be attracted to the Christian way, because they need examples, apprentice-colleagues, to be their companions. Archbishop Justin Welby spelled out that

'this country will not know of the revolutionary love of Christ by church structures or clergy, but by the witness of every single Christian'.[17]

Discipleship is for all, equally, 24/7, and apprenticeship is a great leveller. I shall return later to the whole area of public ministry, about which there is much confused and misleading thinking. For too long we have defined 'church' in terms of its ministry, reducing the scope of the ancient credal description 'apostolic' from its broader, New Testament sense of 'missionary' into details about holy orders, thereby re-defining church in the image of its clergy!

To quote Ray Anderson again,

'Too often, I fear, when the church attempts to make disciples out of Christians by urging them to follow Christ, what is really intended is to mobilize the members of the church to take up church-related ministries and to develop their own interior religious life. A disciple of Christ is not intended to be a little messiah but to participate in the messianic mission to extend the kingdom into every crevice and corner of the world. For the most part, Jesus expected people to live sacramentally in the workplace as disciples of the kingdom rather than become messiahs in their own right. Yet the temptation for the church is to continue to partialize and divide the workplace from its own place in the world by creating disciples whose primary task is to serve the church's existence and mission, not that of the kingdom.'[18]

Confused thinking about 'church' and 'ministry' produces a very upside-down theology! If you want to run a train service you need engineers, track, rolling stock, stations, signallers, platform staff, passengers, and so on. The engine drivers are vital members of the team, but a strategy for a railway company defined almost exclusively around its engine drivers would never even begin to operate. Vital as our public ministers are to the life of the Church, their ministry is contingent on the existence and witness of Christian disciples, the community of the faithful. The sacrament of baptism comes first and is the great leveller.

Our understanding of the nature of discipleship is illuminated by our understanding of what is called 'the priesthood of all believers'. We are priests because Jesus is the high priest; in our baptism we are commissioned as his priests, mediators, reconcilers and intercessors. Martin Luther put it pungently:

'Let every man then who has learnt that he is a Christian recognise what he is, and be certain that we are all equally priests.'[19]

And Bishop Westcott underlined this when he wrote that

'Each Christian in virtue of his fellowship with Christ is now a high priest and is able to come to the very presence of God.'[20]

This is implicit in much of the New Testament and explicit in the first Letter of Peter and the Revelation:

'You also, as living stones, must be built up into a spiritual temple, and form a holy priesthood to offer spiritual sacrifices acceptable to God through Jesus Christ. ... you are a chosen race, a royal priesthood, a dedicated nation, a people claimed by God for his own, to proclaim the glorious deeds of him who has called you out of darkness into his marvellous light.'[21]

'[God] has made of us a royal house to serve as the priests of his God and Father - to him be glory and dominion for ever! Amen. ... You [Lord] have made them a royal house of priests for our God, and they shall reign on earth.'[22]

Our priesthood draws all disciples into the High Priesthood of Christ and is our calling to heal and restore the broken relationships between God and humanity, and between one person and another by the power of his Holy Spirit. It is the disciple's calling to be one who builds bridges in the name of the Lord Jesus, at whose death the curtain that divided us from the presence of God was torn, and age-old racial and religious divisions were broken down.[23]

This 'royal priesthood' - unfettered and unmediated freedom of access to God expressed in faith and baptism[24] - is the root of the tree of faith, planted in the rich soil of discipleship. The whole tree grows from that root and, if the root should die, the tree would die. The whole faith community, the communion of the baptized, those who have heard and obeyed the call of Jesus to be disciples are this 'royal priesthood', called to be Christ's witnesses, to serve him and

'to proclaim the glorious deeds of him who has called you out of darkness into his marvellous light.'[25]

In this respect to concentrate on the clergy is a distraction from the plot; in the words of Robert Horda,

'practically speaking, it is not the pastor who "lets" the congregation in. It is the entire congregation, the church, the faith community which "lets" one of their number, ordained for this purpose, preside.'[26]

Lest someone should think that asserting the primacy of discipleship in the Church is a 'protestant' emphasis, it's worth noting the comments of Pope Francis on ordination as 'one means' by which Jesus serves his people, and that the source of all priesthood is baptism.

'The ministerial priesthood is one means employed by Jesus for the service of his people, yet our great dignity derives from baptism, which is accessible to all. The configuration of the priest to Christ the head - namely, as the principal source of grace - does not imply an exaltation which would set him above others.'[27]

Now let's turn back to the call of Levi, a tax collector who has undoubtedly benefited financially from the political settlement of his day; for Mark this is a convenient story in which to point out Jesus' friendship with doubtful characters.

In the lists of the Twelve[28] provided by Matthew and Mark, Levi is called Matthew. Various theories have been put forward. The one that convinces me is this: there were twelve tribes of Israel[29] in addition to the priestly tribe of Levi which is given special prominence in Jewish thought. So there would be blatant irony for a Jewish author in using this name for a man called after the priestly tribe of Levi, a traitorous tax collector in the service of Herod Antipas (ruler of Galilee), who becomes a disciple of Jesus. It certainly makes the point that the call of Jesus in no way depends on a person's curriculum vitae!

Jesus not only calls this morally pathetic man, he goes to dinner with him and his most unsuitable friends. They were 'people of the land' the 'am ha-aretz' whom common belief put down as cursed by God because they didn't follow his Law. Some were Levi's colleagues in the tax-farming trade. In John's Gospel, the followers of Jesus are described as 'this rabble, which cares nothing for the law, a curse is on them'.[30] By taking a meal with them - in Levi's home (or, intriguingly, perhaps in Jesus' home, because the text just says 'his', which could make Jesus the host, as in a sense he is) - the Lord not only shows courtesy, he demonstrates intimacy with them. [31] For Christians, words like 'church' and 'status' don't sit comfortably in the same sentence. I wonder why the Church allowed itself to adopt titles like, 'Reverend' (deserving of reverence), let alone the added flatteries of 'Very Reverend', 'Right Reverend' and 'Most Reverend', to say nothing of the exorbitant 'Venerable'! These are such obvious and preposterous contradictions of the very heart of our calling to Christ, our identification with the 'people of the land', the outcasts, the ones with whom Jesus had, and still has, so much in common. Little details like religious titles may have deceived us into thinking of the church as an episcopal cloud from which all ecclesial rain falls, rather than as a tree rooted in discipleship. It is possible that a deep-seated democratic reaction to this is what fuelled regrettable developments in our understanding of ministry – of which more anon.

I think of a young priest whose consistent message is that the church must go out to meet people. He remarked,

'People won't walk into our spheres; we need to walk into their spheres. The message of the gospel is healing not only for physical and mental illness but also for spiritual sickness; the church proclaims and practises healing for all three.'

The scholars among the Pharisees took objection to Jesus dining with such obvious sinners. The Pharisees have had a bad press over the years - including the New Testament. They were devoted to the law of God and have tended to be idealised by modern Judaism which derives mainly from them; understandably, the Gospels portray them negatively in the light of first century hostility between Church and Synagogue. It is a mistake to imagine that the Pharisees would have condemned Jesus for caring for outcast people or for relieving suffering; but nothing would have allowed them to compromise the Law of God - that came first, before their neighbours and before themselves. For this reason these men question Jesus' behaviour: 'Why does he eat with such outcasts?' Jesus' answer, which takes the form of a proverb - almost a poetic couplet - is not directly confrontational:

'People who are well do not need a doctor but those who are sick.
I have not come to call respectable people, but outcasts.'[32]

Initially, his opponents may have taken some comfort from these words - they don't see that they themselves have a problem with sin, so Jesus' remarks don't at first hearing appear to concern them. The irony is hidden inside the whole story of the ministry of Jesus as it unfolds, the big picture of Mark's Gospel. The inability of the Pharisees to recognise Jesus' positive attitude towards legally-unrighteous people becomes a major factor in leading them to reject him. Those who consider themselves to be in good spiritual health are, in fact, desperately sick, and those who know themselves to be outcast - one might say 'infected' - are healed and welcomed to the banquet of the Messiah.

This is puzzling to those who haven't followed through the story of Jesus, who haven't perceived the contradictions inherent in the accounts of his birth - the Son of God laid in an animal's feeding trough, the Word pitching his divine tent in humanity, a refugee Messiah - nor struggled with the teachings of this Rabbi who takes seriously the Scriptures on the one hand, and challenges the heart of human motivation on the other. Christian discipleship is a conundrum to those who have not been stunned to silence by the events of his suffering, death and resurrection, what St Paul calls 'God's folly' and 'the foolish message of the cross'.[33]

The expression 'the mystery of the gospel' is used in the New Testament letters[34] as we may today describe the cure for a disease that had in the past evaded researchers but has now been discovered. The implication is that the good news of Christ remains puzzling to many, and there is bound to be something puzzling about his disciples. Becoming one of his disciples is the point at which these contradictions begin to make sense in those who have accepted the challenge to follow Jesus and are discovering what forgiveness cost him.

There used to be an advertisement for the *Alpha* course showing someone carrying a big question mark, implying that people who want to make sense of a confusing world and confusing lives should join an Alpha group. My image of a Christian disciple is of someone wearing a T-shirt with a big question-mark on it. It is more important than ever that Christian disciples should be puzzling, Christian conundrums, question-mark people. If we are living as the apprentices of Jesus, our lives will not quite add-up. Witnessing with integrity means living in such a way that one's life cannot make sense unless God exists. Yes, we eat and sleep and work and laugh and cry and reproduce like everyone else, but some things won't make sense - and I don't mean just how we spend Sunday mornings! Our values will be different, our level of compassion will be different, the way we make judgements will be different, and people will notice. They may not say anything for a very long time - perhaps years - then, one day, the question will come out, 'Why are you like that?' That's what I mean by being question-mark people.

Brian MacLaren has written:

'If Christianity isn't the quest for (or defense of) the perfect belief system ("the church of the last detail"), then what's left? In the emerging culture, I believe it will be "Christianity as a way of life", or "Christianity as a path of spiritual formation".

'The switch suggests a change in the questions people are asking. Instead of "How can I be right in my belief so I can go to heaven?" the new question seems to be "How can we live life to the full so God's will is done on earth as it is in heaven?" Instead of "If you were to die tonight, do you know for certain that you would spend eternity with God in heaven?" the new question seems to be "If you live for another thirty years, what kind of person will you become?"

'I'm not certain any postmodern churches exist quite yet. But even in modern churches we can feel a rising tension, a fomenting discontent: Why aren't we making better disciples? Why aren't people becoming more holy, joyful, peaceful, content and Christ-like? Why … are so few of our good Christian people good Christians? Why is Prozac needed by so many? Why are the most biblically-knowledgeable so often so mean-spirited? Why are our pastors dejected so often? Why do our speakers (both human and electronic) have to blare so loudly to get a response, and even then, why is the response so shallow or temporary?

'That discontent may be the ending point for many of us, but it is the starting point for our brothers and sisters of the emerging culture. If Christianity doesn't bear fruit in a way or rhythm or pattern of life that yields Christ-likeness in real measure, they aren't interested. Being "saved" is suspect if people aren't being transformed.'[35]

Our society is characterised today by expanding institutions (company mergers, state regulation of every aspect of life) and by growing self-interest (*my* car, *my* holiday, *my* rights) - we get bigger and greedier. So who is left to build real communities for real people, communities which both support and challenge human life? Answer: the community of the good news, the Church, disciples, us, who live, not for the sake of that community, but for the good news which that community embodies. In other words, it's you and me, the disciples of Christ, who are the good news for society today.

If the Church is to make a difference for good in today's 'emerging culture' - not in the first instance for its own good but for love of the world God loves so deeply - it needs authenticity and integrity in all its members. The Church needs to be what she claims to be, the community of Jesus' disciples, the people who have accepted the call to follow him. Which also means that if there's a problem with the Church, the buck stops right here with you and me. What we are determines how the gospel will be received, and proves or disproves its authenticity.

One of Archbishop Rowan Williams' brilliant little sayings is, 'Church is what happens when the impact of Jesus draws people together.' I have taken something for granted to this point in describing the calling of 'disciples' (plural). Whether we are all together in one place or dispersed as Christ's witnesses, we're not called into an isolated spiritual existence but into a fellowship of disciples, a band of people who live in every corner of the world, who are not even divided by death, and who express this real belonging to one another in the local community of faith. It's appropriate that the biblical word we translate as 'fellowship' is more accurately translated 'communion'; this leads us into lots of other closely associated words like 'community' and 'commune'. And it's no accident that we use the word 'communicate' for the act of receiving Holy Communion because this is the very epicentre of what we mean by the fellowship or communion of the Holy Spirit.

A twentieth century theologian, P.T. Forsyth, pleaded for a bigger vision of the Church, based on the work of Christ for the whole human race:

'It was the race that Christ redeemed, and not a mere bouquet of believers.'[36]

We're not a bunch of blooming lovelies bundled together to look and smell nice, all arranged in an ecclesiastical vase! There is something closer and more fundamental in our communion with one another, even though we are called by Christ for most our lives into diverse different spheres of witness to him.

Being a disciple is about being a Christian, a servant of God, all the time and in every place. I believe there is a basic misunderstanding of one of the key illustrations of the Church in the New Testament: the body of Christ. Most liturgical worship uses a ceremony known as 'the Peace'. It's a stylised form of the ancient and widespread greeting in Jewish and Christian tradition - indeed, in many other cultures, too. It has often been the liturgical fashion to preface the Peace with a slightly distorted biblical reference to the body of Christ, as in: 'We are the body of Christ. In the one Spirit we were all baptized into one body ...' This was followed by encouraging congregations to greet one another and share the Peace - all good stuff. I wonder whether emphasising our belonging to the body of Christ just at the point of sharing with one another did some damage to our psyche because, subliminally, it turned us in on ourselves and gave us an unhealthy sense of the body of Christ principally as a gathered body ministering to itself. We began to say to ourselves, 'We here are the body of Christ; it is only while we celebrate the Christian family meal together that we express what it means to be his body. We are the eucharistic community and the Church exists to meet our spiritual needs.' In other words, being together is what we mean by 'our common life'. Such un-expressed, sub-conscious thinking can be highly deceptive.

That is not to denigrate either the importance of the body of Christ gathered in worship or the need to supply the needs of her members. However, I am sure that Saint Paul[37] intended a broader reference than the local gathering for worship; he was describing the great diversity of life and witness of the Christian community during all 168 hours of the week. So, what will you be doing on Monday morning?

John is in the factory, Jane is in the hospital, Joe is in school, Arun is visiting a client, Maria is opening her shop, Clare is looking for a job, and so on: that's what the body of Christ looks like for almost all the week. The body of Christ is, for most of the time, turned outwards, explosively diverse in her mission, witness and discipleship; it's 'making Christ visible'.

Jesus Christ calls us into a community of disciples we call the Church, a body that exists both when it meets together and when it is scattered and explosively present in the wider community. Like the first disciples we are called to be with him, doing what he is doing, learning to be like him, bringing the kingdom into the here and now and making it available.

For some time I have been haunted by the question 'What is the Church for?' It started when I took up a post as a national church officer. My family and I found ourselves in a non-parsonage house for the first time in nearly three decades; our neighbours were a young family with two children. One day, when I was cutting the grass in the front garden, the wife and mother from next door started chatting and said she'd heard I was 'a kind of vicar'. I explained as best I could. Then she asked me a question no one had ever asked me before: 'What's the Church for?'

Some people are puzzled at the thought of the question even being asked, but the Church cannot be an end in itself. I'm sure you won't be surprised to know what some of its members think:
· It's there for me and my soul's comfort
· It's there to get me to heaven.
· It's there because I've put money and effort into it.
· It's there because it needs to be until I'm in the churchyard.
· It's there in order to get more members.
· It's there to preserve a building.
· It's there to be serious or fun or relevant or musical or cool or a refuge or whatever I want it to be.

Trustees of charitable bodies are obliged to demonstrate that their charities have a genuine purpose. This 'demonstration of public benefit' is found in the Gospels. In John's Gospel chapter 15, where Jesus makes comments about bearing fruit, he's forcing us to ask: 'What on earth is the Church for?' Unquestionably, the Church's priorities beyond worship lie outside her walls. An introverted church is a sham, not a church at all, because it doesn't attempt to live up to God's own priorities. A church that's bothered about itself - about the needs of its congregation, about its buildings, about its size, about its petty squabbles, even about its own salvation - is preaching a badly distorted un-gospel.

Even though we know gathering to praise God is a priority, it's easy not to put worship first in the life of the Church because 'going to church' and living the Christian life are not always the same thing. For a moment, let's think about worship in the sense of adoration, giving back to God as much as our feeble minds and hearts are capable of. The Shorter Westminster Catechism of 1646-7 famously describes 'man's chief end' as 'to glorify God and enjoy him for ever'. I firmly believe worship comes first before everything else.

Archbishop Justin Welby's introduction to the Lambeth Lecture on Evangelism[38] affirmed this when he said,

'I want to start by saying just two simple sentences about the Church. First, the Church exists to worship God in Jesus Christ.'

But it was the two sentences that followed that were widely shared in the cloud:

'Second, the Church exists to make new disciples of Jesus Christ; everything else is decoration. Some of it may be very necessary, useful, or wonderful decoration – but it's decoration.'

The tweeting and re-tweeting of those two sentences (omitting the word 'Second') implies that the tweeters consider 'searching for the kingdom of God',[39] for example, is 'decoration'! If the Church's only un-decorative purpose after worship were to make more disciples it would become an organism whose true purpose is simply to reproduce and we would be left with a host of unanswerable questions about the gospel. There is nothing wrong with church growth – quite the opposite, it's vital and worth putting a lot of effort into – but what's it for? Surely it must be more than 'a population drive for heaven'![40] The Archbishop continued,

'The best decision anyone can ever make, at any point in life, in any circumstances, whoever they are, wherever they are, whatever they are, is to become a disciple of Jesus Christ. There is no better decision for a human being in this life, any human being.'

Amen to that!

So, what *is* the Church for? One answer is because God created it. The confession of Peter that Jesus is 'the Christ, the Son of the living God'[41] is the rock on which the Church is built; the source of her life is the in-breathed and outpoured Holy Spirit; she is the body and bride of Christ; her agenda is the Lord's commission to the apostles.

However, that's not really to answer the question posed by my neighbour. The more straightforward answer is clear: the Church is for God and for the world. The Church is for God because he is and we worship him, expressing this in faith, prayer, the word, the sacraments and service. The Church is for the world because that's where God's heart is - it's what 'God so loved'.[42] All this is focussed on Jesus Christ and the Father's gift of the Spirit who brings the risen Christ to us and breathes into us Christ's love and mercy. What we are determines how the gospel will be received.

The purpose of the Church, the fellowship of the disciples of Jesus, is God and people. 'Simples!' God and people is the purpose of the whole body, as well as every particular organ of it. Since the whole church is the whole body of Christ's disciples, we are people *for God*, and people *for others.*

Increasingly, the culture of 'church', particularly in those churches that are old and hard of hearing, is alien to most people. Most people do not customarily gather on Sunday mornings to sing in chorus with others, handling books (let alone several of them), sitting on wooden benches in cool buildings, sometimes being ignored as if by a supermarket checkout-assistant chatting to a colleague or alternatively being pestered as if by an over-enthusiastic sales-assistant, not knowing whether to sit down or stand up, often being glared at, and so on. These cultural norms make for a difficult or even impossible transition for a disciple of Jesus from a fresh expression of Church to what has often in the past been thought of as normal, and must force the older tradition to examine how it expresses what happens when the impact of Jesus draws people together. A major difficulty is that people who have been immersed in a particular style of church worship for many years find it difficult to assess what is of the essence and what can, and sometimes must, be left behind. When churches feel under pressure – financially, numerically, in age profile, for instance – their natural tendency is to emphasise what gives them reassurance, and that is often not the essence but the culturally conditioned aspects. Thus the language and music of worship become battle-grounds, and some new disciples walk away – as any sensible person should. There is much more work to be done on helping older churches to see themselves as others see them.

The well-known early medical missionary in Central Africa, Albert Schweitzer, once said that

'I know one thing: the only ones among you who will be really happy are those who have sought and found how to serve.'[43]

That has strong resonances for me of the call on Jesus' disciples to be willing to take up the cross. For Simon Peter, Andrew and Levi this call was to a radical change that would affect the whole of their lives. An individual who simply responds to a call and then does nothing with it is not what the Bible describes as a disciple. Apprentices are learners of the craft of being Christian, taught on-the-job by the Master to whom we are all bound in the relationship of calling and response.

Jesus not only calls us to come; he commands us all to follow, to be his witnesses 24/7.

'Attachment to the Church without discipleship is the husk without the kernel,'

wrote Emil Brunner.[44] The Church in the future must to a far greater degree than in the recent past be the community of the gospel personified in those who are called as question-mark disciples.

God of power,
you have called us as disciples of your Son:
may the boldness of the Spirit transform us,
the gentleness of the Spirit lead us,
and the gifts of the Spirit equip us
to serve and worship you;
through Jesus Christ our Lord.
Amen.

(A prayer for the Guidance of the Holy Spirit)

Ten Signposts
for helping disciples make Christ visible[45]

The Church is called to ...

1. celebrate the discipleship of all baptized believers

2. practise the best possible nurture, growth and development for disciples

3. support the lifelong journey of disciples

4. affirm the importance of discipleship in daily living

5. encourage disciples to see the whole of life as a calling from God

6. equip disciples to lead others to Christ

7. identify and develop appropriate gifts for leadership in every sphere of life

8. form policies that encourage disciples

9. commit resources to supporting discipleship

10. encourage fresh thinking, innovation and experiment in discipleship

References

1. James Catford in interview with Stephen R Holmes, in The Bible in Transmission, 2002.
2. Mark 1. 16-18; 2. 13-17
3. Mark 1. 14, 15; 3. 14,15.
4. Disciples Together, SCM, 2014.
5. Evangelii Gaudium / The Joy of the Gospel, CTS, 2013, p 63.
6. 1 Corinthians 7. 17.
7. Colossians 1. 27.
8. Matthew 10. 5-15ff.
9. For instance, Romans 1. 5; 1. 7; 1. 13.
10. For instance, Acts 6. 1, 7; 9. 2; 11. 26.
11. Matthew 28. 19, 20; Mark 16. 15; John 20. 20-22; see also Luke 24. 47 and Acts 1. 4-9.
12. Luke 1. 1-4; John 21. 25.
13. Matthew 14. 22-32.

14. John 18. 15-18, 25-27; 21. 15-19.
15. Man in the Midst, Highway, 1955.
16. An Emergent Theology for Emerging Churches, B.R.F., 2007.
17. Lambeth Lecture 5.3.2015.
18. ibid.
19. The Babylonian Captivity of the Church.
20. B.F. Westcott: The Epistle to the Hebrews, Macmillan, 1892, on Hebrews 10. 19.
21. 1 Peter 2. 5, 9.
22. Revelation 1. 6; 5. 10.
23. Mark 15. 38 etc; Ephesians 2. 14-18; Hebrews 10. 19-21.
24. Ephesians 3. 12.
25. 1 Peter 2. 9.
26. Strong, Loving and Wise, The Liturgical Conference, 1987.
27. Evangelii Gaudium [The Joy of the Gospel], CTS, 2013, p 55.
28. Matthew 9. 9; 10. 1-4; Mark 3. 16-18.
29. Joseph's tribe was split into Ephraim and Manasseh.
30. John 7. 49.
31. See John 1. 38, 39; Revelation 3. 20.
32. Mark 2. 16, 17.
33. 1 Corinthians 1.18-31.
34. For example: Ephesians 6. 19; Colossians 1. 26, 27; 2. 2; 4. 3.
35. Brian D McLaren: Emerging Values in the Leadership Journal, Summer 2003
36. The Church and the Sacraments, 1916.
37. In Romans 12, 1 Corinthians 12 and Ephesians 4.
38. Lambeth Lecture 05.03.2015.
39. See Luke 4. 16-21; 7. 18-23.
40. D.T. Niles.
41. Matthew 16. 16.
42. John 3. 16, 17.
43. Speech to students of Silcoates and Ackworth Schools, Wakefield, 03.12.1935.
44. The Letter to the Romans, 1938, on Romans 2.
45. Adapted from a Church of England General Synod paper.

4 Called to Christ

During a recent sermon, I asked a congregation, 'What's the most important difference between the Christian faith and other major religions?' Silence! At first they thought it was a rhetorical question, then, after a few shots-in-the-dark, someone said, 'Christ.' Correct. It was obvious really but curiously easy to forget. What is it about Jesus Christ that is so central to being disciples? It's who he is, what he has done and why that matters.

Jesus calls us to follow, not a system of belief, not even in the first instance a way of life, but himself; it is for him that countless numbers have given their lives over two millennia. Although Jesus Christ himself could not be said to have founded any religion, the Christian gospel is focussed on him as Lord and God. The person and work of the Lord Jesus Christ and the worship his disciples offer him, rather than his teaching, important though that is, is the content of the gospel. In the words of Evelyn Underhill (1875-1941),

'The primary declaration of Christianity is not "This do!" but "This happened".'[1]

In other words, it is not the moral demand 'God wishes it' (*deus vult*), but the gift of forgiveness, 'God does it' (*deus facit*).

Jesus was a Hebrew rabbi, yet it is not what he was but who he is that constitutes the Christian faith and is the basis of its declaration of hope. When Buddha lay dying, he told his disciples to follow no leader but to make his teaching their light because it was his teaching, not his person, that mattered:

'Unflinchingly, ardently and resolutely you should apply yourselves to gain your own salvation.'

I hope that this will not be mis-represented as an attack on the integrity of Buddhism: I am merely observing that Buddhist discipleship is centred on teaching, Christian discipleship on a Person. It is interesting, however, to note that statues of the Buddha are at the heart of Buddhist devotion in its various forms. With Jesus it is his person and what he has done that take the priority over his teaching.

'The supreme object of the Christian faith is thus the person of Jesus himself; no one theology or system of doctrine must be identified with the Christian religion,' wrote Alan Richardson. 'Historical Christianity (the mainstream of the development of Christian thought) ... is consequently not a system of ideas, but an attitude towards a certain historical person; and for this reason it is not possible or desirable for us to attempt to separate the religion of Jesus from the religion about Jesus. For the content of the Gospel is Jesus himself, not a creed or a doctrine or a theory about him.'[2]

In the early centuries of the Church's life two key doctrines were argued about and even fought over: the Trinity and the Person of Christ. Even the list of what constituted the Hebrew Scriptures (the Old Testament) was not confirmed in the early decades of the Christian Era, and it took until AD 367 for the first list of New Testament books as we know them today to appear.[3] An outsider might simply say that all these were arguments between theologians with too little to do, but that would be unfair because it was and is important to understand these vital matters on which the Christian hope rests. It was as though the Scriptures of the Old Testament and the Apostolic writings, along with their experience of Jesus Christ and the power of the Holy Spirit, were all being poured into a crucible heated violently by persecution and politics.

The process of working out what really had been revealed and achieved by God in Christ was heated and passionate, but eventually Christians came to an explanation that fits the evidence and their experience, and that translates into many cultures, however curious that explanation may appear to some. Rowland Hill put it simply:

'...a particular man who lived in Palestine two thousand years ago, worked as a carpenter at Nazareth, then exercised a special ministry of teaching and healing for three years, was framed by his enemies, unjustly tried and executed by crucifixion - that man was, in fact, God Almighty. ...
And so we say that a certain baby in a cot in a house at Nazareth was God Almighty; that some kid at the local school at Nazareth shared a desk with God Almighty; that somebody who broke the leg of his chair took it round the corner to the carpenter's shop and had it mended by God Almighty. It's an odd thought, isn't it? Yet it was the people who lived with Christ who came to believe this about him.'[4]

There is no direct credal statement in the New Testament of the Three-in-One God, Father, Son and Holy Spirit[5] but the underlying doctrinal evidence is so solidly embedded there that it found expression remarkably early in the Church's life, and the Apostle Paul could take a nascent form of trinitarianism for granted.[6] Richard Bauckham has helpfully commented that 'the story of God's acting and suffering in the world in the gospel story of Jesus is trinitarian in form. That God is trinitarian emerges, as it were, from the story. A doctrine of the Trinity represents what we need to say about God in himself for the biblical story about God to be a true story. It is authorized by the story in that it follows from taking the story seriously as authoritative metanarrative.'[7]

The three-fold baptismal formula in Jesus' final commission to his Apostles,

'Go therefore to all nations and make them my disciples; baptize them in the name of the Father and the Son and the Holy Spirit'[8]

would have been known before it was included in St Matthew's Gospel less than half a century after the resurrection. Its three-fold importance lies first in being an early form of trinitarian statement, second in commissioning the Church in mission, and third because it rapidly became the basis of the baptismal covenant for new disciples of Christ and created a framework for evangelism and Christian formation.

A detailed doctrinal understanding of the person of Jesus Christ - that the eternal Word of God took on human nature, and that his perfect divinity and humanity are united in one person - was thrashed out from the New Testament evidence[9] in the fourth century and resulted in the final version of the Nicene Creed. It was neatly put by Edward Taylor, a seventeenth century poet:

'God's only Son doth hug Humanity Into his very Person'.[10]

Worship of the one God in three Persons is central to the Christian confession, to baptism and to discipleship. Small wonder that many Christians are confused when approached by sects who claim that there is no biblical evidence for the Trinity or for worship of the God-Man. Where, then, is the evidence and why is the evidence important? Let's look at a few examples.

Very early in the life of the early Church, Paul wrote to the church at Philippi, probably quoting a hymn to Christ that these Christians already knew:

'He was in the form of God; yet he laid no claim to equality with God, but made himself nothing, assuming the form of a slave. Bearing the human likeness, sharing the human lot, he humbled himself, and was obedient, even to the point of death, death on a cross! Therefore God raised him to the heights and bestowed on him the name above all names, that at the name of Jesus every knee should bow - in heaven, on earth, and in the depths - and every tongue acclaim, "Jesus Christ is Lord," to the glory of God the Father.'[11]

We can recognise in this passage thinking that is still being developed. At this very early stage of reflection on who Christ is, the author of the hymn said no more than that Christ was 'in the form of God' but 'made himself nothing' or 'emptied himself' of all that distanced God from humanity; that he was 'obedient to death' and 'God raised him to the heights'. St Paul himself, using his own words, writing to the Church at Colossae at much the same time, was more explicit when he said,

'It is in Christ that the Godhead in all its fullness dwells embodied.'[12]

The Letter to the Hebrews (which may well be a collection of sermons) begins by setting out the foundation doctrine for the whole work:

'God has appointed his Son heir of all things; and through him he created the universe. He is the radiance of God's glory, the stamp of God's very being, and he sustains the universe by his word of power. When he had brought about purification from sins, he took his seat at the right hand of God's Majesty on high, raised as far above the angels as the title he has inherited is superior to theirs.'[13]

This resonates with the description of the Lord as 'our great God and Saviour Christ Jesus' in the Letter to Titus.[14] Let's leave St John's Gospel, the most important evidence, to later in this chapter.

Moving on in the church's story, Polycarp, a second century bishop of Smyrna (Izmir), was executed around AD 156 during one of the periods of intense persecution of Christians, probably for refusing to offer incense on a pagan altar. Christians had made their commitment to Christ in the words of the earliest Christian creed, 'Jesus is Lord',[15] and therefore could not offer the same obedience to the Emperor or some other pagan god. He said,

'Eighty-six years I have served him and he has done me no wrong. How can I blaspheme my King and my Saviour?'[16]

There is something in this experience of Christ in the lives of the first few generations of Christian disciples and in their witness that, combined with the apostolic writings of the New Testament, provides us with a message which remains as powerful today as ever.

So, our response to the call to be a disciple is a commitment to the Lord Jesus Christ, the only Son of God and total human being like no other; it is not simply a decision to follow the Christian way. Christ himself is the content of the good news, which is why the New Testament is less a receptacle for doctrinal statements and more the tale of how women, men and children have been called by Christ and become his disciples. I recall a highbrow television series looking at belief in God, at the end of which the presenter made some comment like this:

'You can argue for and against belief in God and no one can ever prove the case either way, except, perhaps, for the person who says, "I know God exists; I spoke to him this morning." '

It is thus we turn to a remarkable story that forms the whole of chapter 9 of St John's Gospel, the healing of a man who had been blind from birth. It is a story that takes us round in a circle from a question about sin and blindness to a conclusion about blindness and sin. Today we rightly have proper sensitivities about the allegorical use of words like 'blind' but, please forgive me, this is inevitable in looking at passages such as this which come to us from a far less sensitive age.

John sets his Gospel in the context of a series of festivals. At the Feast of Tabernacles,[17] there were two great ceremonies in Jerusalem. One was the drawing of water from the Pool of Siloam; the water was carried to the Temple with Psalms of praise and poured around the altar - 'With joy you shall draw water from the wells of deliverance'[18] - a reminder of the water which came from the rock in the wilderness at the time when the people of Israel had been rescued from slavery in Egypt. And the other ceremony was the lighting of special lamps in the Temple - 'a pillar of cloud by day and of fire by night',[19] a reminder of the leading of God throughout those years of wilderness wanderings. So, when Jesus is recorded as saying,

'Whoever is thirsty should come to me and drink. Whoever believes in me, streams of life-giving water will pour out from his heart' and 'I am the light of the world. Whoever follows me will have the light of life and will never walk in darkness',[20]

we immediately see the connections. It was at the festival of Tabernacles that the controversy over this crucial question of who Jesus is and where he had come from began to develop, questions so crucial to the author and readers of the fourth Gospel.

John takes an extreme example here, a man who was congenitally blind, and his disciples pose the classic rabbinic question, a moral theologian's puzzle:

'Whose sin caused him to be born blind? Was it his own or his parents' sin?'

It was a genuine question from their perspective: was the blindness a punishment for some sin of the man's parents before he was born, or was the sin innate in the man *in utero*? Jesus' reply might seem puzzling and even offensive: 'He is blind so that God's power might be seen at work in him.'[21] This is a heavy hint about what the reader will come across later in this gospel when, from the end of chapter 12, the gospel moves forward to what is sometimes described as 'The book of Glory', in which the glory of the Son of Man is revealed in his betrayal and suffering, and that, through his suffering, God's glory is revealed.[22]

Using spittle, which was itself thought to have healing properties, Jesus puts mud on the man's eyes and tells him to go and wash in the Pool of Siloam, the name of which means 'sent'. Over the years, I've asked congregations to tell me what they understand by that word 'sent' in this story. (I've even had answers about perfume!) For John the word is loaded with meaning, a constant reminder of the One who had been 'sent'. The Evangelist has massive affirmations to make of Jesus Christ as the Father's missionary, from the moment the Gospel begins to its end. The Prologue refers to the creating Word of God from the beginning

> 'through him all things came to be ... In him was life, and that life was the light of mankind ... So the Word became flesh; he made his home among us, and we saw his glory, such glory as befits the Father's only Son, full of grace and truth.'[23]

The question of where Jesus comes from runs as a constant theme throughout the Gospel.[24] So, when the blind man is told to wash in the waters of the 'sent', what are we to think? If we haven't got the message in reading the first eight chapters, here it is underlined: salvation, healing, deliverance comes by washing in the One who was sent by the Father, God's missionary-Son.

Apart from the important clear reference to baptism (and probably also to anointing), the blind man's 'washing' in Christ is offered to the reader in various other images in St John's Gospel. At the beginning, the writer uses words to describe holding on to Jesus as a shipwrecked person might hold on to a life-raft:

> 'all who did accept him, to those who put their trust in him, he gave the right to become children of God.'[25]

The best known pair of verses in the Bible describe this as faith, in the sense of trust and foundational belief:

> 'God so loved the world that he gave his only Son, that everyone who has faith in him may not perish but have eternal life. It was not to judge the world that God sent his Son into the world, but that through him the world might be saved.'[26]

Similarly, towards the end, the purpose of the Gospel is summarised as being written

'in order that you may believe that Jesus is the Christ, the Son of God, and that through this faith you may have life by his name.'[27]

Again and again the writer directs our attention to Jesus as the object of saving faith.

Back to the story of the blind man. The controversy surrounding the healing begins with the man's neighbours, who are quizzed as to the facts of the case as far as they can tell. Their witness is confused, some think it's the same man who can now see, others think it can't be. The man speaks up: 'It's me, all right!' He tells them the story but he has no idea where Jesus is because, of course, he used to be blind so he doesn't know what Jesus looks like, and also he was down at Siloam when he regained his sight and Jesus wasn't.

The situation rapidly escalated into a major issue as advocates of the Law of God hauled the man before our old friends the Pharisees who interrogated him about what happened and raised a religious question about Sabbath observance. The Pharisees couldn't object to a healing on the Sabbath unless someone had contravened the Law. But there was something they could nail him for: Jesus made mud with spittle; that qualifies as making bricks, just on a different scale. Gotcha! Working on the day of rest.

Don't dismiss this. For Jesus' contemporaries, he had broken the fourth Commandment. The writer is forcing us to ask ourselves whether curing blindness is more important than the Law, even if it happens this way and on a Sabbath? It's no small wonder that Christians have had trouble for 2,000 years balancing the relative importance of law and grace, the given and the contextual, 'the old and the new'[28] because we are committed to a paradox: to take the whole of God's revelation seriously - not cutting out the bits we find unpalatable - while at the same time interpreting it for the present moment, in this place and in the light of the gospel of grace. The ever-present paradox in this story is put before us in Jesus' Sermon on the Mount,[29] in the controversies surrounding St Paul's mission among gentiles, and in many ethical dilemmas facing Christians today. It is all too easy for Christians to adopt the attitude that all questions must be answered with a definite opinion, whereas the gospel persistently challenges us to face up to paradoxes and grey areas. The uniqueness of the Christian revelation is that the gospel of grace is spoken on the lips of the Son of God himself, but this can often make moral questions even more complicated.

These issues are also live for other faiths and their holy books; it's no less an issue for Jews with the Hebrew Scriptures or for Moslems with the Qur'an. Take an example from the Qur'an. On the one hand, it says,

'We decreed to the Children of Israel that if anyone kills a person ... it is as if he kills all mankind, while if he saves a life it is as if he saves the life of all mankind.'

And, on the other,

'Those who wage war against God and His Messenger and strive to spread corruption in the land should be punished by death, crucifixion, the amputation of an alternate hand and foot, or banishment from the land: a disgrace for them in this world, and a terrible punishment in the Hereafter.'[30]

Using the ancient scriptures of any religion in order to back up prejudices (literally pre-formed judgements) is no way to search for truth. It is useful to recognise that this is not an uniquely Christian challenge.

Now the dispute in the gospel story of the blind man moves to an investigation by the religious authorities, with the man's parents and the man himself called as witnesses. It gets nowhere: the facts are there and the parents won't commit themselves because they are scared of the thought-police. These authorities, who appear by now to have accepted the healing as a physical fact, challenge the man forcibly:

'Promise before God that you will tell the truth! We know that this man who cured you is a sinner,'
He replies, 'I do not know if he is a sinner or not. One thing I do know: I was blind and now I see.'[31]

Yet the irrefutable proof is standing before them. This discussion has become like the impossible one of proving the existence of God. The difficulty faced by the Pharisees is that they have no conception of Jesus other than as a rabbi around whom remarkable things seem to happen. The Gospel has taken us to the place where what we do not yet know about Christ far exceeds what we might know; and the question about who Jesus is surfaces again and again.

The antagonists get rattled when the man's impatience gets the better of him:

'Why do you want to hear it again? Do you also want to become his disciples?[32]

From that point, the authorities wash their hands of the man and offer insults in place of reason.

'You are that fellow's disciple; but we are Moses' disciples. We know that God spoke to Moses; as for that fellow, however, we do not even know where he comes from!'[33]

Yes, John, we take the hint again. They don't know where Jesus comes from, but we've been reading your Gospel and you're making it clear where he comes from, because it lies behind the big question - 'Who is Jesus?' - to which you've already alerted your readers many times.[34] 'You,' the authorities say to the man, 'are that fellow's disciple.' At the heart of understanding discipleship is knowing whose disciples we are. We are the disciples of the fellow who says to us, 'Come follow me!'

That's why the question 'Who is Jesus - not just for us but for everyone?' is so crucially important in our secular and multi-faith world. Archbishop Rowan Williams commented that Christians are not in a religious marketplace in which we barter argument and conviction in an attempt to 'get a bargain' but must show total commitment both to the God revealed in Jesus and also to those whom he invites, that is to all with whom we are in dialogue about faith. Is Jesus a prophet? Is he Son of God and Son of Man? Is he the Father's missionary, the creating Word? Is he the 'Lord' of the creeds and, as St Paul would have it,

'the visible likeness of the invisible God ... through whom God created everything ... and reconciled all things to himself'?[35]

Those who are 'this fellow's disciples', will affirm these titles. Other faiths will answer the questions in a variety of ways. Does that mean we regard Jesus as one among a shelf-full of historically significant body-mind-and-spirit figures? What on earth would the New Testament writers make of the times in which we live, a world of apparently competing major religions, a world where ethnicity and religion are often inextricably combined? I suspect they might notice how like the world of their own day it is and how complex the world of religious belief can be.

This identity question is personalised in the 'I am ...' sayings of Jesus in the Fourth Gospel, powerful not only because they take us back to that unutterable YHWH word given to Moses,[36] and because, like an Advent calendar, each of them opens a door into a new dimension of the nature of Jesus Christ. Twice we read, 'I am the light of the world'; elsewhere 'I am the bread ... I am the life ... I am the door ... I am the good shepherd ... I am the resurrection and the life ... I am the vine', and perhaps the most revealing, 'I am the way, the truth and the life; no one comes to the Father except by me.'[37]

This final declaration is key to understanding who Jesus claims to be. We could argue about whether it means that by Christ everyone may come to the Father, or that none may come to the Father except by Christ, or maybe a bit of both! What there can be no argument about is the focus on Christ alone at the centre in this picture of salvation. In the conversation that leads up to this statement the disciple Thomas (the archetypal sceptic) thought he had asked the Master for directions to heaven, a spiritual map, a philosophy, a sacred ritual, or a holy book. But the answer the Lord gave him was, 'It's me! I am in my own person the way to the Father, the truth who brings together mind and reality in a single person, the vital energy of life' (that we may have noticed before in the Gospel). The call to discipleship is the call to Christ and Christ alone.

Jesus finds the once-blind man, who now recognises Jesus not simply by sight but by insight, and the man kneels to worship the eternal Word, the missionary-Son of the Father, the great 'I am', whom we as readers can believe without seeing, the Master, Lord and God. In a multi-confessional and secular world, can we say that today? I believe we can, and it has immense consequences.

More than a century ago Bishop Westcott[38] called the ejection of the healed man from the synagogue and the man falling on his knees before Jesus 'the beginning of a new Society' in which 'the Lord offers Himself as the object of faith' to the whole human race as the Son of Man. The man who now can see worships Christ. Jesus himself is the new truth, and obeying his call is the new confession that forms the basis of the new society. Indeed, many scholars believe this conversation between the man and Jesus is an echo of the professions of faith used in first century baptismal rites. Christian disciples are called by Christ and their ultimate purpose is Christ. In the journey of St John's Gospel, by chapter nine we have been led to Jesus Christ as the One in whom we put our trust. From this point onwards we cannot pretend to ignore the challenge to become his disciples, not simply followers but worshippers. It will lead us to a crescendo of faith and worship after the resurrection, culminating in the declaration 'My Lord and my God!' – and that's Thomas again.[39]

All this is of a piece with the healed man's kneeling before Jesus and worshipping him.

'Do not think that Christ is found in ceremonies, in doctrines kept after a fashion, and in constitutions of the church,' wrote Erasmus, priest and scholar, in 1516. 'Who is truly a Christian? Not he who is baptized or anointed or who attends church. It is rather the person who has embraced Christ in the innermost feelings of his heart, and who follows Him by his holy deeds.'[40]

Such Christ-centredness is sometimes a challenge to traditional 'church'. Most emphatically in our own time it is a challenge to 'secular religion', and is equally a call to engage seriously with people of other faiths. Some think that the question 'Who is Jesus Christ?' is academic theology. Far from it! Jesus Christ, by whom we have been called, whose disciples we are, is himself the challenge to face up to the critical faith issues that confront society every day in our relationships, in the street and increasingly in the media.

The centrality of Jesus in the Christian way can never be simply a doctrine. Because he is the person we proclaim, Jesus Christ himself must always be at the centre, however difficult that is to get across in an age when the big stories that offer universal meaning are rejected in favour of individually-tailored notions that have meaning 'just for me'. Not so the gospel: we are called to take the good news to all because it is for all.

Ebenezer Erskine (1680-1754), a rather dour Scots cleric (to whom I am distantly related, though he was no friend of bishops!) put it neatly in one of his sermons:

'He is the centre of doctrine; there is not a word in the Bible but it points towards Christ, as the needle in the compass points to the pole star. He is the centre of worship; the prayers and praises of all believers terminate in Him.'[41]

Sharing the gospel of the one Lord among atheists is, in some respects, the least challenging task. Certainly, the lines of demarcation are reasonably clear: is the Christian faith what it claims to be or is Jesus Christ and the faith he inspires a fantastic delusion? It is more difficult to engage with people of other faiths, as undoubtedly we are called to do, not least because the faith principle is appreciated, and the risk of unwitting offence is greater. Therefore we approach evangelism among people of other faiths by both honouring their tradition and appreciating what their faith perceives of the one God, while at the same time retaining our own integrity as disciples who are bound in covenantal love with the 'one Lord, Jesus Christ'.[42]

Those who are older will be unlikely to have had the benefit of a grounding in the basic tenets of major world religions that younger generations have had in school. It may be at a very basic level but there is a real sense in which the future of the planet - certainly in terms of international relations - will depend on an understanding of and respect for the great world religions. It is easy for those with no appreciation of other religions to bundle together those who hold a faith peaceably with the few who are militant fundamentalists.

Christian faith itself is widely misunderstood: in the 'global north' it is scorned as regressive, repressive and judgemental; and in many other regions as the source of a self-centred abandonment of moral values. It's easy to see how both of these came about: for instance, upholding standards in sex and relationships has led to Christians being viewed as negative; and including all comers without imposing religious codes has led to the Christian faith being blamed for the abandonment of moral standards. So it's a lesson for people of all religions - and for agnostics and atheists - that the future of civilisation lies in better understanding of world religions.

One of the blessings of churches that are 'established' either by law or custom is that they can provide an open and non-threatening space for different denominations and faiths to engage with one another. The bishop who ordained me presbyter once described these ancient churches as bridges, built across barriers to be trampled over in the process of bringing together people and places. He was not implying that the bridge has no strength in itself, no convictions of its own, but that grace and history established the bridge-church in such a place that it can be a meeting place both for Christian denominations and world faiths.

The New Testament writers knew nothing of the ancient religions of the east, nor of Islam, whose origins lie in the sixth century AD; their experience was of Judaism and pagan religions, but the principles outlined by St Paul at various points in his Letter to the Romans[43] help us understand a vital principle in inter-faith relationships:

'Scripture says, "No one who has faith in him will be put to shame": there is no distinction between Jew and Greek, because the same Lord is Lord of all, and has riches enough for all who call on him. For "Everyone who calls on the name of the Lord will be saved." '

The Apostle affirms that all seeking after God is a search for the living God, regardless of in whose name that search is conducted. Since there is only one Lord, he argues, then all religious search is a search for the same Lord. So are we to understand that Paul was advocating a syncretistic view of religion, 'All shall win and all shall have prizes'?[44] Certainly not. There is a radical difference between searching and finding, as the verse that follows makes clear:

'But how could they call on him without having faith in him? And how could they have faith without having heard of him? And how could they hear without someone to spread the news?'[45]

The obligation to share the good news lies with us. Paul writes consistently of 'faith in him', not faith in a system but in a person, the Lord Jesus Christ, and on many occasions he describes Christians as people who are 'in Christ'. So the Christian disciple respectfully brings to any conversation with people of other faiths, not a system or a religious package, but a person, a Saviour and a Lord.

At the end of John chapter 9 the story moves back to its starting-point.[46] Jesus reminds his audience of the original question, 'Who sinned?' But now old values have been turned upside-down. The blind can see, and those who think they see with their eyes prove to have no insight at all, they are truly blind. It's not about doctrine.

Alan Richardson, who was referred to early in this chapter, put it neatly:

'What the believer possesses as a result of his conversion is not a set of formulae which he can repeat like a parrot, nor a system of doctrines which he accepts as infallibly true, nor a book of oracles out of which he can answer every question: he possesses new eyes.'[47]

It's all about *'this fellow'*, Jesus Christ the Lord, the one whose apprentices we are.

Eternal God,
whose Son Jesus Christ is the way, the truth, and the life:
grant us to walk in his way,
to rejoice in his truth,
and to share his risen life;
who is alive and reigns, now and for ever.
Amen.

(A prayer for use in Easter-tide)

References

1. Worship, Harper, 1936 & 1957.
2. Creeds in the Making, SCM, 1935, chapter 1.
3. In The Letter of Athanasius.
4. I Believe and Trust, Mowbray, 1992.
5. What Alec Ryrie described as "the British Reformation's most resolutely non-barking dog": Being protestant in Reformation Britain, OUP 2013.
6. For instance, 1 Corinthians 12. 3-6.
7. Scripture and Authority Today - Grove Biblical Series 12. *A metanarrative is a story that sums up human existence and applies to all people at all times.*
8. Matthew 28. 19.
9. For instance, John 1. 1, 18; 20. 28; Colossians 2. 9; Titus 2. 13; Hebrews 1. 8, 10;

etc.

10. 1642-1729. My Blood is Drinke indeed: Meditation on John 6. 55
11. Philippians 2. 6-11.
12. Colossians 2. 9.
13. Hebrews 1. 2-4.
14. Titus 2. 13.
15. 1 Corinthians 12. 2,3.
16. The Martyrdom of Polycarp, Tr. J.B. Lightfoot.
17. See John 7.
18. Isaiah 12. 3.
19. Exodus 13. 22; etc.
20. John 7. 37, 38; 8. 12.
21. Verses 2, 3.
22. John 13. 31; etc.
23. John 1. 1-18.
24. John 3. 13, 31, 34; 5. 37; 6. 29, 33, 41, 42; etc.
25. John 1. 12.
26. John 3. 16, 17.
27. John 20. 31.
28. Matthew 13. 52.
29. Matthew chapters 5-7.
30. Qur'an 5. 32, 33; translated by M.A.S. Abdel Haleem, Oxford, 2004.
31. Verses 24, 25.
32. Verse 27.
33. Verses 28, 29.
34. For example, John 1. 1-4, 10-14, 16-18.
35. Colossians 2. 15, 16, 20.
36. As we have seen, 'I am' is one possible translation of YHWH.
37. John 14. 6.
38. Commentary on John's Gospel, 1881.
39. John 20. 8, 16, 28.
40. The Education of a Christian Prince.
41. Sermon delivered in 1729.
42. The Nicene Creed.
43. See Romans 2. 12-16 in particular.
44. Lewis Carroll: Alice's Adventures in Wonderland.
45. Romans 10. 11-14.
46. Verses 39-41.
47. ibid.

5 Called to the Cross

What would you say most people in the street think that Christian faith is all about? Many people today won't be able to answer at all. Some might say, 'Christians believe in God; Christians say you should love your neighbour.' Naturally, both these answers would depend on how much of the language of faith has been picked up. For those who are able to supply more detail, Jesus Christ would feature in the response, often first as a teacher, then, perhaps, they might add something about Christmas, and that he died on the cross. Martin Luther once observed:

'If you want to understand the Christian message you must start with the wounds of Christ.'

Ask the person in the street about the Church and there may be reference to a building or to clergy, especially if there's been any kind of scandal in the media! Pursue this enquiry into whether they have any experience of what the Church does and it's more than likely that, if there is an answer, it will be about some evangelistic activity rather than involvement in society. That in itself is not a bad sign because the Church is not only called to be visible as 'light'' but also to be the hidden ingredients of 'salt' and 'yeast'. [2]

What evidence is there in the apostolic age to tell us about what the first Christians believed? Let's look at this under two headings: the Christian confession (what did they mean by 'I believe'?) and the content of the gospel (what did they believe in?). The earliest 'creed' seems to be clear from what the Apostle Paul wrote in his First Letter to the Corinthians and his Letter to the Romans:

'I must impress upon you that no one who says "A curse on Jesus!" can be speaking under the influence of the Spirit of God; and no one can say "Jesus is Lord!" except under the influence of the Holy Spirit.' [3]
'If the confession "Jesus is Lord" is on your lips, and the faith that God raised him from the dead is in your heart, you will find salvation.' [4]

That statement of faith, 'Jesus is Lord', was for the earliest Christians both a personal confession of faith in the Lordship of Christ - 'Jesus is my Lord' - which for many led directly to their deaths, and also a confession of public truth, truth for all, whether anyone else believes it or not – 'Jesus is the Lord'. As can be seen from the Letter to the Romans above, the confession of faith and the content of the gospel are inextricably linked.

The content of the gospel amounts to a number of key facts about the One who is the object of the confession of faith: Jesus Christ. Essentially, the incarnation, cross and resurrection of Christ are explicitly the core content of the gospel. For instance, St Paul writes,

'And now, my friends, I must remind you of the gospel that I preached to you; the gospel which you received, on which you have taken your stand, and which is now bringing you salvation. ... First and foremost, I handed on to you the tradition I had received: that Christ died for our sins, in accordance with the scriptures; that he was buried; that he was raised to life on the third day, in accordance with the scriptures; and that he appeared to Cephas [Peter], and afterwards to the Twelve. Then he appeared to over five hundred of our brothers at once, most of whom are still alive, though some have died. ... This is what we all proclaim, and this is what you believed.'[5]

Luke's Gospel includes the stories of the birth and childhood of Jesus, and John's Gospel explores the meaning of the Word taking flesh, but all four gospels spend very significant proportions of their accounts on the events of the last eight days of his earthly ministry. Matthew begins to refer to Jesus' death in chapter 16 (of 28), Mark first mentions his death at the beginning of chapter 3 (of 16), Luke has Jesus and his disciples heading for a climax in Jerusalem in chapter 9 (of 24), and in John, Jesus' death and resurrection permeate most of the Gospel (of 21 chapters). It is very clear that, in the first Christian century, the central facts of the earthly life of Jesus, and in particular his cross and resurrection, were the content of the gospel.

This emphasis on the cross and resurrection of Jesus did not weaken during the early centuries of the Church's life. During the second and third centuries a creed developed that, by AD 390, became known as 'The Apostles' Creed'. This is very much a personal confession of faith for use in baptism, and is written in the first person, 'I believe in God ...' Of the eighteen lines in the creed, ten are statements about events concerning Jesus Christ. The other two creeds, the 'Nicene' and 'Athanasian', from the fourth and fifth centuries, similarly concentrate on Jesus Christ – both who he is and what he has done for humanity - the one in whom Christian disciples place their trust. Jesus Christ is the gospel.

For the twenty-first century, the Church of England decided to authorise various alternative affirmations of faith, one of which (written with all-age worship in mind) refers to Jesus in these terms:

'We believe in God the Son,
who lives in our hearts through faith,
and fills us with his love.[6]

There's a clear reference to the Letter to the Ephesians[7] but no mention of the historic acts of God in Christ, in particular his birth, death and resurrection. The feel of this affirmation is warm and assuring but it lacks the key ingredient of Christian affirmation, rootedness in history.

So how does the gospel affect the way that disciples live? How might that make an impact for good on the society in which we live? The person in the street might answer that it's the Sermon on the Mount or some other ethical teaching of Jesus that would most affect the way disciples live. But that's not what the Church for two millennia has affirmed and proclaimed as the heart of the gospel; something prior to ethical teaching affects the way disciples live. Christian moral values are a stream that flows from the source, and the source is the person of Jesus Christ and what he has done for the whole created order.

In Mark's version of the story, closely followed by Matthew and Luke, Jesus was in the north-west of the area he and his disciples tramped around, near Caesarea Philippi, when, apparently without warning,

'on the way he asked his disciples, "Who do people say I am?" They answered, "Some say John the Baptist, others Elijah, others one of the prophets." "And you," he asked, "who do you say I am?" Peter replied: "You are the Messiah." Then he gave them strict orders not to tell anyone about him; and he began to teach them that the Son of Man had to endure great suffering, and to be rejected by the elders, chief priests, and scribes; to be put to death, and to rise again three days afterwards. He spoke about it plainly. At this Peter took hold of him and began to rebuke him. But Jesus, turning and looking at his disciples, rebuked Peter. "Out of my sight, Satan!" he said. "You think as men think, not as God thinks." '[8]

The question was a challenge to the heart of their faith, 'We all know what the crowds think of me. Some think one thing, some another. What about you?' This question can't have been included by the Evangelists just as a scene-setter for Peter's answer. The Evangelists (authors of the gospels) were deliberately writing for the future – how far ahead, they did not know – unlike the Apostle Paul and others whose letters were addressed in the first instance to their contemporaries. So we always ask the Evangelists, 'Why did you include this?' The stories are there for the reader to ponder and answer, and they lead us to what is still the first question in evangelism: 'Who do you think Jesus is? - a teacher? – God? – a fraud?' The way you answer that question leads into faith or away from it. Peter answers in terms of his Jewish upbringing, 'You are the Messiah,' in other words, 'You're the King, the Boss, the Anointed One that our people have been waiting for.' In terms that both Gentile and Jewish Christians would soon understand it in Corinth, Rome, Nairobi and Cardiff, 'You are the Lord.'

It's clear by this point in the Gospels that there was already a celebrity culture developing around Jesus, not least because of the miraculous healings and the feeding of thousands of people that had recently taken place. Once Peter's confession had been uttered the danger increased. That's something every age knows about, and now both the mass media and social media have turned 'celeb' culture into a religion. This look-at-me age pleads with us to set ourselves up as bigger and greater and more capable and more beautiful and more – you name it – than we actually are; and Christians are not immune (though when they fall for it the results are inevitably tragic).

Now in our story even the disciples might have started to treat Jesus in a way that denied his humanity, and it is his humanity that will be most obvious in his sufferings and death. Scholars have puzzled about what reasons Judas Iscariot may have given himself for betraying Jesus. Was it that, like Peter at this point, he could not face the prospect of a suffering Messiah and hoped to provoke Jesus into a demonstration of power? Jesus' immediate instruction to the disciples not to tell anyone about him – an injunction that appears frequently in Mark's Gospel – was wiser than it might appear.

From this point the story moves geographically towards Jerusalem and spiritually in two directions: towards suffering and glory. Once the light has begun to dawn about who Jesus is, he can move on to teach about his suffering, death, and resurrection, and his glory will be revealed in transfiguration. The teaching about coming rejection by the leaders of their own people must have been hard enough, let alone trying to explain his suffering, and that he would be killed. At this moment, Jesus is known to be a worker of miracles and great teacher, now recognised as Messiah. The very idea of becoming a voluntary murder victim would be crazy. But the predictions are even more weird: 'rise again three days afterwards'? That's completely off-the-scale, beyond comprehension, sheer fantasy! So Peter tries to call Jesus back to his sense of reality, receives one of the sternest of rebukes by Jesus and finds himself called 'the enemy'. Peter and the others must learn that the way of the Son of Man is the way of the cross, and it will be the way the disciples must be willing to walk, too. Remember why Matthew, Mark and Luke included this story at a crucial point in the narrative – because they wanted us to stand there with the first disciples, so Jesus is speaking to us. The way of the cross and resurrection is the direction all disciples must be ready to walk.

The path by which humanity is saved is Christ's rejection, suffering, death and resurrection. The path to be taken by disciples is similar: being willing to stand against the flow, experiencing true repentance that turns over the heart as a plough turns over soil, dying to all that is sinful, and finding new life here and hereafter. No one will ever make sense of the Christian faith without being willing to walk the path of suffering, death and resurrection. Peter, James and John begin to grasp this, which seems to be why they can be led on to an experience of God's glory in Jesus' transfiguration.

Meanwhile, Jesus turns to the crowds. Why do the writers bother telling us about this change of audience? Perhaps because, by the time they're are writing this down, the Church is beginning to lose its first love and take God's grace for granted. Discipleship on the cheap is blasphemy; faith is a relationship which is never dictated on our terms. So the writers make a point that there is no credible witness to Christ without this experience of dying and rising because the cross is both the sign and the measure of value.

'Then he called the people to him, as well as his disciples, and said to them, "Anyone who wants to be a follower of mine must renounce self; he must take up his cross and follow me." '9

It is interesting that, while Matthew records this statement in exactly the same way as Mark, Luke adds 'daily', as in 'take up his cross daily'. This suggests that, by the time and place in which Luke was writing his account, taking up the cross may already have become a well-known expression and its meaning had begun to be spiritualised. Christian disciples must indeed take up their cross daily, though 'daily' inevitably softens the brutality of what it meant to be crucified by the Romans in the first century A.D.

As it stands in the Gospels of Matthew and Mark, this is an astounding statement, and one blunted by so much familiarity, or by so many hymns and songs that have innocently sucked out its meaning over the years, or by so much talk of a sore toe that is 'my cross to bear'! It is so easy to con myself into believing that I am in fact carrying my cross until someone assaults my faith and I realise that self-important insecurity lurks behind all pious appearance. Richard MacKenna commented,

'It is the cross-bearers, the failed, the broken, the empty, unlovely, unprestigious, unglamorous, who are the real body of Christ. No resurrection without crucifixion, no life without death first - the Christian paradoxes at the heart of the gospel - but we are terrified to put them into practice because in our heart of hearts we believe that the folly of the cross **is** folly; we pay lip service to it, but never dare light the blue touch-paper."[10]

What does it mean, then, to take up our cross daily? In one respect that is an impossible question to answer because each of us is an individual in an unique time and place. But it may be worth attempting to discover some principles by looking at what it meant for Jesus.

'The cross means that God refuses to verify himself. "Let the Christ, the King of Israel, come down now from the cross, that we may see and believe." But he stays where he is."[11]

The cross that Jesus bore was not a symbol of power in any normal meaning of the word, but a sign that God's power is known through weakness. Corinth in the first century AD was a cosmopolitan city at the heart of Mediterranean trade routes, home to the Temple of Aphrodite, goddess of sexual love, a city where power mattered. It was hard for the early Corinthian converts to break the habits of a lifetime. In his Second Letter to the Corinthians the Apostle Paul seems to have been addressing folk who found power-in-weakness difficult to grasp. He writes:

'If boasting there must be, I will boast of the things that show up my weakness. ... I will not boast on my own account, except of my weaknesses. ... [The Lord's] answer was: "My grace is all you need; power is most fully seen in weakness." I am therefore happy to boast of my weaknesses, because then the power of Christ will rest upon me. So I am content with a life of weakness, insult, hardship, persecution, and distress, all for Christ's sake; for when I am weak, then I am strong."[12]

The universal sign of Christian faith, the cross, says it all. Walter Bruegemann makes an interesting link between the distinctive call of the people of Israel (the burning bush, the giving of the law) and our call to be disciples:

'The requirements of covenant are exhibited in the public ministry of Jesus and in his summons to discipleship. As Israel is called at Sinai to a distinct identity, so Christ's call to discipleship is a summons to join his alternative practice of reality. Because his summons contests the dominant regime (the empire of Rome), he was executed (crucifixion) by the empire through which the dominant narrative has its Friday moment of prevailing."[13]

We have forged crosses of precious metals to make them beautiful and inspiring, but the cross on which our Lord was crucified was ugly, painful and led even him to cry out in dereliction.[14] We have boasted of the pain of carrying the cross and boosted our self-righteousness – not that anyone with much sense ought to be impressed! At other times we have trivialised the cross and gone on our jolly way rejoicing.

This temptation, to make the cross of Jesus more acceptable, is particularly strong at a time when Christians develop a minority complex. When you feel that the majority is against you, you may be anxious not to put any obstacles in the path of future disciples, so the view of the Christian life you portray is unduly optimistic. In this context, you also find great support in being close to your fellow-disciples, so you may be tempted to use worship as a celebratory drug and become so spaced-out that you'll sing anything with a good tune, regardless of the words! In one of Charles Wesley's great autobiographical hymns the first three verses express the spiritual birth-pangs of a disciple – a crucifixion – that the poet was experiencing in the year 1738:

And can it be that I should gain
An interest in the Saviour's blood?
Died He for me, who caused His pain -
For me, who Him to death pursued?
Amazing love! How can it be,
That Thou, my God, shouldst die for me? ...

'Tis mystery all: th'Immortal dies;
Who can explore His strange design? ...

He left His Father's throne above
So free, so infinite His grace -
Emptied Himself of all but love,
And bled for Adam's helpless race.

Nearly a century after this was written, Thomas Campbell wrote the gloriously exuberant tune 'Sagina' with which the hymn is almost invariably associated, but which musically destroys the profound solemnity of this depiction of the incarnation and crucifixion in these three verses, particularly when congregations sing them as though they've had a skin-full in the pub on a Saturday night! Of course, the remaining verses are joyful and entirely suited to the tune, so perhaps the hymn should be sung to two tunes!

My chains fell off, my heart was free,
I rose, went forth, and followed Thee. ...
No condemnation now I dread;
Jesus, and all in Him, is mine ...

All that can be said of the call of Jesus to renounce self and take up the cross is how the Gospels describe the events of the crucial three days, from the last supper and the garden of Gethsemane to the garden of the tomb and the first supper of resurrection: desolate, deserted, alone, a helpless victim, in agony of body and spirit, crucified. George MacLeod, founder of the Iona Community, wrote that

'Jesus was not crucified in a cathedral between two candles, but on a cross between two thieves; on the town garbage heap, at a crossroads so cosmopolitan they had to write His title in Hebrew, Latin, and Greek. At the kind of place where cynics talk smut, and thieves curse, and soldiers gamble, because that is where He died and that is what he died about and that is where churchmen ought to be and what churchmen should be about.'[5]

That is the disciples' way, the natural way for disciples. It is not possible to be a faithful witness to the Crucified, nor truly to discover the joy of his resurrection until you know the pain of the cross.

In helping young disciples I have sometimes found it useful to describe the way to faith as **A B C D**. Coming to Christ, we ...

Admit that we're sinners and need those broken relationships with God and others to be fixed;
Believe in Jesus Christ, God's only Son, the Saviour and the Lord;
Count the cost of discipleship - the cost of the cross; and
Do something about it.

It's the third letter (C) that Jesus is describing here: counting the cost of being a disciple, at whatever radical cost. A couple of the parables that Luke attaches to this teaching put the point neatly.

'No one who does not carry his cross and come with me can be a disciple of mine. Would any of you think of building a tower without first sitting down and calculating the cost, to see whether he could afford to finish it? Otherwise, if he has laid its foundation and then is unable to complete it, everyone who sees it will laugh at him. "There goes the man", they will say, "who started to build and could not finish." Or what king will march to battle against another king, without first sitting down to consider whether with ten thousand men he can face an enemy coming to meet him with twenty thousand? If he cannot, then, long before the enemy approaches, he sends envoys and asks for terms. So also, if you are not prepared to leave all your possessions behind, you cannot be my disciples."[16]

Matthew, Mark and Luke all follow up what Jesus says about carrying the cross with what looks at first sight like an explanation:

'Jesus said, "Whoever wants to save his life will lose it, but whoever loses his life for my sake and for the gospel's will save it. What does anyone gain by winning the whole world at the cost of his life? What can he give to buy his life back? If anyone is ashamed of me and my words in this wicked and godless age, the Son of Man will be ashamed of him, when he comes in the glory of his Father with the holy angels." '[17]

That word translated 'life', or sometimes 'soul', is literally 'breath', we might call it 'the vital spark of human existence'. Without losing your very being, you can never find the real purpose of your existence. And the meaning behind life, that which underlies all existence, is the cross of Jesus which he shares with his disciples. These scary words of Jesus are followed by a profound saying and the most intriguing riddle of the gospel about losing and redeeming life.

So what's the answer to the riddle? What can you give to buy back your life? Jesus doesn't provide an answer. Is it 'nothing'? No, not nothing. When you think about it, the only currency that can be used to pay for your life is, simply, your life. There is nothing at all but the very spark of your human existence that can equal the value of your life.

Contemporary society is not radically different from the society in which Jesus preached. The scale of success and acquisition is greater today but the human heart and mind is still deeply addicted to achievement, success and personal prosperity. What is your most important goal in life? – your most extravagant dream? - even the purest and most lovely desire? Is there anything you could give in exchange for the gift of your life? Is there any coinage, material or spiritual, that could pay for your life or mine? When Jesus calls you and me to follow him and to be willing to carry his cross daily, he asks for one thing only: our lives. The disciple is one who has responded to this call to give away our lives to him whose cross we bear, whose own life was exchanged for ours, whose resurrection transforms old life to new.

Which love is greater? God's love for us, or our love for God which we circumscribe with inconveniences, and may, if we're honest, be much weaker than we like to suppose. But God knows this. If faith is centred on the quality or quantity of love we can give to God – or what we think we can spare! – Christ will take second place at best; it's the bear-trap of faith, the obsession with how well we can believe. But if our faith is centred on God's love for us, then we find ourselves immersed in an all-encompassing divine embrace seen perfectly in the wounded hands of the risen Jesus holding the whole creation. In the words of the song, it's not, 'Father, we love you …' but, 'Father, you love us.'

Such divine love inexorably leads us to the cross – not the little upsets of life, not even the great tragedies of the world - but the cross of Christ which he invites us to carry and, in so doing, to lose our own lives in his life.

Christopher Marlowe (who was no saint) turned the ancient story of Faustus into a play about Renaissance man.[18] Dr Faustus has no fear of God, hell or Lucifer – 'This word damnation terrifies not him' - and does a deal with the Devil: his life in exchange for 24 years of having whatever he desires. Yet all his desires disappoint him and, before he knows it, the years have run out:

> 'Stand still, you ever-moving spheres of heaven,
> That time may cease, and midnight never come.
> … that Faustus may repent and save his soul.'

Faustus thinks there is a price-tag on life – until it is to be taken away.

The Gospels follow the conversation about counting the value of life with the story of the transfiguration. Peter, James and John accompany Jesus up a mountain where his body is transfigured with glory, the disciples see a vision of Moses and Elijah, and hear the divine voice, 'This is my beloved Son, listen to him.'[19] The disciples are confused: Jesus had spoken of his death and they had only half heard. If only they had listened! Now they have seen a vision of glory and Jesus tells them to say nothing until the Son of Man has been raised from the dead. The three disciples have been shown that Jesus' progress towards the cross is not simply a drift towards a tragically unfortunate outcome. From now on they will learn that carrying the cross is entirely consistent with the glory of the Son – they have been shown the end before the beginning. However fallibly, they are being prepared to carry the cross and therefore to be ambassadors of his resurrection.

The inextricable bond between cross and glory can be illustrated in that curious incident related in the Fourth Gospel when Judas Iscariot receives the bread dipped in the common dish. John tells us,

> 'It was night. When he [Judas] had gone out, Jesus said, "Now the Son of Man is glorified, and in him God is glorified." '[20]

The glorification of the Son of Man leads to our transfiguration, a product of the sacramental life, and both sacraments of the gospel (Baptism and the Supper) orbit around the cross and resurrection, such that we find ourselves caught up in Christ's suffering, death and glory. Transfiguration is the purpose of the sacraments, and disciples live in what some have called the 'rhythm' of community, word and sacrament.

Baptism, the liturgical beginning of the Christian pilgrimage, is not simply a ceremony with water performed in the Name of God but it is the act that formally commits us to Jesus' sacrificial life. His baptism of suffering is ours and our baptism seals that connection. Mark provides an account of an encounter between Jesus, James and John, when the sons of Zebedee approached him and said,

> ' "Teacher, we should like you to do us a favour." "What is it you want me to do for you?" he asked. They answered, "Allow us to sit with you in your glory, one at your right hand and the other at your left." Jesus said to them, "You do not understand what you are asking. Can you drink the cup that I drink, or be baptized with the baptism I am baptized with?" "We can," they answered. Jesus said, "The cup that I drink you shall drink, and the baptism I am baptized with shall be your baptism; but to sit on my right or on my left is not for me to grant; that honour is for those to whom it has already been assigned." '[21]

At the end of the same chapter, as if to bring this home, Mark tells us that when Jesus heals Bartimaeus, a blind beggar, 'at once he recovered his sight and followed him on the road.'[22] The Evangelist has told us several times that Jesus and his companions were on the road to Jerusalem where Jesus would face suffering death and resurrection. Bartimaeus therefore becomes a practical example of courageous, sacrificial discipleship.

We are powerfully reminded by Matthew Mark and Luke of 'the cup that I drink' in the agonised prayer in the Garden of Gethsemane,[23] yet there is more to teach us in the encounter with James and John. Though Matthew's account omits the references to baptism, the passage has strong sacramental overtones both for Baptism and the Eucharist - even the way Mark renders the conversation sounds like what we know of the earliest Christian liturgies of baptism. We are reminded that there are sacrificial consequences for all Christian people who share in celebrating the sacraments.

Because baptism is a crucial element of discipleship, preparation for baptism – the catechumenate - in the early life of the Church often took place over months or years. It began with an enrolment ceremony that involved candidates being marked on the forehead with Christ's signature, the cross, a sign of his claim on human life and a clear display of the link between taking up the cross and discipleship. After preparation, when the baptism took place, often at Easter, the candidates were presented almost naked; they were buried in the water and brought up again in resurrection, clothed in white garments, often anointed with fragrant oil, and made ready to celebrate the cross and resurrection around the Lord's table among his people. Small wonder that baptism and the sign of the cross, with their symbolism of death, resurrection and glory, were so important in the life of the Church and remain so significant today.

'Have you forgotten that when we were baptized into union with Christ Jesus we were baptized into his death? By that baptism into his death we were buried with him, in order that, as Christ was raised from the dead by the glorious power of the Father, so also we might set out on a new life.'[24]

'Baptized into union with him, you have all put on Christ like a garment.'[25]

Alexander Schmemann encapsulated bringing together the Easter message of baptism, eucharist and promise of glory:

'Baptism, by its very form and elements - the water of the baptismal font, the oil of christmation refers us inescapably to "matter", to the world, to the cosmos. In the early Church the celebration of baptism took place during the solemn Easter vigil, and in fact, the Easter liturgy grew out of the "Paschal mystery" of baptism. This means that baptism was understood as having a direct meaning for the "new time", of which Easter is the celebration and the manifestation. And finally, baptism and chrismation were always fulfilled in the Eucharist - which is the sacrament of the Church's ascension to the Kingdom, the sacrament of the "world to come".'[26]

Christians have argued for most of two millenia about how we understand the link between the eucharist and the cross. St Paul, in chapters 10 and 11 of his First Letter to the Corinthians, not only gives us what is probably the earliest account of the institution of the Lord's Supper but applies its symbolism to the nature of the Church: each disciple not only shares in the body and blood of Christ by eating bread and drinking wine but is also a broken fragment of the body of Christ.

'When we bless the cup of blessing, is it not a means of sharing in the blood of Christ? When we break the bread, is it not a means of sharing in the body of Christ? Because there is one loaf, we, though many, are one body; for it is one loaf of which we all partake.'[27]

Sometimes Anglicans like me make a big fuss about sharing from one cup in Communion (as contrasted with individual cups) but unthinkingly consent in many churches to eating individual wafer-breads that bear no sign of their having been broken from 'one loaf'. The image is so clear and powerful: when you tear apart the 'loaf' (for St Paul that may have been unleavened but that's of no significance here), each piece is unique, just as every one of us is an unique member of the body of Christ, the Church. Were you to have the time and patience, you could put all the pieces together because the individual fragments make up a single loaf. The cup over which we give thanks to God and from which we share the blood of Christ is filled not with individual doses but the mélange of grapes trodden, fermented and shared – just like our lives. The sip I take is indistinguishable from the sip you take: we dwell in Christ and he in us.

'As Jesus meets with his friends for that last supper and tells them to see the broken bread and wine poured out as his body and blood which are about to be broken and poured out in crucifixion, he says in effect, "What is going to happen to me, the suffering and death I'm about to endure, the tearing of my flesh and the shedding of my blood, is to be the final, the definitive, sign of God's welcome and God's mercy." Instead of being the ultimate tragedy and disaster, it is an open door into the welcome of the Father. That is what he is saying in the upper room on Maundy Thursday, and that is what he says every time we celebrate the Eucharist in commemoration of his death; in affirmation of his resurrection; in expectation of his coming again.'[28]

Discipleship is the transfigured life initiated by baptism and sustained by the eucharist for God's mission in his world.   Both sacraments of baptism and communion drew Peter, James and John, and still today draw the disciples of Jesus into his cross, his resurrection and his glory.

Almighty God,
whose most dear Son went not up to joy
but first he suffered pain,
and entered not into glory before he was crucified:
mercifully grant that we,
walking in the way of the cross,
may find it none other than the way of life and peace;
through Jesus Christ your Son our Lord.
Amen.

(Collect of the 3rd Sunday of Lent)

References

1. Matthew 5. 14-16; 6. 22-23; Mark 4. 21, 22; Luke 8. 16; 11. 33-36; John 8. 12; 12. 36, 46.
2. Matthew 5. 13; 13. 33; Mark 9. 50; Luke 13. 20, 21; 14. 34.
3. 1 Corinthians 12. 3.
4. Romans 10. 9.
5. 1 Corinthians 15. 1-6, 11b.
6. Michael Perry: Church Family Worship, 1986, Jubilate Hymns.
7. Ephesians 3. 14-19
8. Mark 8. 27b-33.
9. Mark 8. 34; Matthew 16. 24; Luke 9. 23.
10. God for Nothing, Churchman 1984/5.
11. C.K. Barrett: sermon in 1968, quoting Mark 15. 32.
12. 2 Corinthians 11. 30; 12. 5, 9, 10.
13. The Practice of Prophetic Imagination, Fortress, 2012.
14. Mark 15. 34; etc.
15. Only One Way Left, Iona Community, 1956.
16. Luke 14. 27-33.
17. Mark 8. 35-38.
18. First performed between 1588 and 1593.
19. Mark 9. 7b.
20. John 13. 30b, 31.
21. Mark 10. 35-40; see also Matthew 20. 20-28.
22. Mark10. 52.
23. Matthew 26. 42; Mark 14. 36; Luke 22. 42.
24. Romans 6. 3, 4.
25. Galatians 3. 27.

26. Alexander Schmemann: For the Life of the World - Sacraments and Orthodoxy (1963, 1973).
27. 1 Corinthians 10. 16, 17.
28. Archbishop Rowan Williams: Being Christian, SPCK, 2014, p 47.

6 Called to be Changed

Churchgoers sometimes complain to their pastors, 'This is not the church I joined years ago!' to which there is only one reply: 'This is not the world you joined years ago!'

Change is not new. It can be complex, frustrating, confusing and often appear unnecessary. When Henry Ford started producing motor cars some people told him that all they needed was faster horses. We live in a world of accelerating change. All God's grace is needed to follow the one Lord, Jesus Christ in lifelong discipleship in this complex, changing, multi-faith and multi-cultural world. Being a disciple puts us at the centre of change and development, as it did for the first disciples of Jesus. More than ever we need to pray for confidence to accept the things that should not change, courage to change the things that should, and the wisdom to know the difference.[1]

Our discipleship needs to be radical or no one else will be changed. Unfortunately, the prevailing image of the Church is of an organisation locked in the past and unable to get out. What might be its last seven words? 'We've never done it that way before!' Some Christians are scared to the point of neurosis about change because they have not understood the distinction between what is unchanging and what must change. Of course, we must reckon with the power of nostalgia - I can remember the emotional pain of seeing a new building erected on the site of a demolished church that had meant something special to me in the past - but I am convinced that the passion with which some Christians fight against change as though it were a threat reveals a more serious and worrying sickness, an inability to rest in the certainty of God's unchanging love, life and grace. A night prayer calls us to 'rest on God's eternal changelessness'.

Scott Peck comments that anything that is alive changes:

'All life is process. And since I choose to have a living God, I believe that my God is also in process, learning and growing and perhaps even laughing and dancing.'[2]

Even if I don't 'choose … my God', we get his point. In page after page of the Bible we read of God responding to the predicaments into which we put him. He is the God who constantly brings harmony out of the disharmony of our lives.

In the Revelation, we read of the song of the living creatures round the throne of God:

'Holy, holy, holy is God the sovereign Lord of all, who was, and is, and is to come!'[3]

The past ('was') and the present ('is') our minds can cope with, but that God 'is to come', that there is yet something more of God in the future, is mind-blowing. This sense of living in three modes of time is acted out in the eucharist, the Christian family meal. The celebration takes us back to the example and command of Jesus, and to his cross and resurrection; it brings the past into the present through the process of sharing together a sacred meal; and it anticipates the heavenly banquet when all will be fulfilled. The nature of God does not change, but that he is the God of change cannot be challenged. So how does this relate to discipleship?

First, discipleship is a lifelong apprenticeship, a change of gear into a new occupation. For the first disciples in the Gospels it was a process of growth in understanding, a learning experience typified by the journey taken by Jesus and his companions towards Jerusalem that occupies most of Luke's account.[4] Matthew employs a more subtle approach to the learning process by dividing the teaching of Jesus into five blocks, reminiscent for his Jewish readership of the five books of Moses, the Torah. He describes Jesus' method of teaching-practice-reflection, and repeatedly the Master challenges the disciples with paradoxes: 'You have heard ... but I say'. Discipleship is a learning experience.

Second, discipleship in the Gospels involved abandoning self and belonging to a new community. When Jesus called his first disciples he was doing what was natural for a rabbi of his time and place, gathering around himself a learning community. In terms of commitment such a community would often take priority over one's own family. We can find this in a number of places in the Gospel accounts, such as in the question of who constituted Jesus' family:

'Then his mother and his brothers arrived; they stayed outside and sent in a message asking him to come out to them. A crowd was sitting round him when word was brought that his mother and brothers were outside asking for him. "Who are my mother and my brothers?" he replied. And looking round at those who were sitting in the circle about him he said, "Here are my mother and my brothers. Whoever does the will of God is my brother and sister and mother." '[5]

His hard saying about letting the dead bury their dead also needs to be read in this context of community and, in both of the instances in which it occurs,[6] particularly the one in Luke's Gospel, there is a clear reference to the cost of discipleship:

'As they were going along the road a man said to him, 'I will follow you wherever you go.' Jesus answered, "Foxes have their holes and birds their roosts; but the Son of Man has nowhere to lay his head." To another he said, "Follow me," but the man replied, "Let me first go and bury my father." Jesus said, "Leave the dead to bury their dead; you must go and announce the kingdom of God." Yet another said, "I will follow you, sir; but let me first say goodbye to my people at home." To him Jesus said, "No one who sets his hand to the plough and then looks back is fit for the kingdom of God." '

Third, the first disciples experienced a radical change in their personal circumstances, both literally and spiritually. This call to a total change of life is anticipated by the radical nature of John the Baptist's preaching and the clarity of Jesus' message:

'After John had been arrested, Jesus came into Galilee proclaiming the gospel of God: "The time has arrived; the kingdom of God is upon you. Repent, and believe the gospel." '7

It is what we might call the 'religious' aspects of faith that can sustain us through change. By and large across our churches 'religion' is neglected. Here's a paradox. It has become a commonplace to say that 'religion is unbelief'8 in the sense that belief is an encounter with the person of Jesus Christ, whereas religion is merely an attempt to search for him by our own efforts. In that sense, undoubtedly religion is unbelief. Yet, once encountered, there are important Christian religious activities that help to sustain the relationship with the Lord, activities such as prayer, participation in the life of the Church, Bible reading, worship, self-examination, and so on. Regrettably, even in the most lively churches of all traditions, these religious aspects of our relationship with Christ are frequently side-lined. When members of the Church regard them as optional extras to faith, rather than as the joys and duties that flow from faith, we are soon left with biblically illiterate and spiritually infantilized disciples who pray when they need something and go to church if they haven't anything more pressing to do: discipleship becomes a pastime. Small wonder that so many in our churches are insecure in the changelessness of God, and consequently fearful of change in small matters that are of far less significance.

On the other hand, there are Christians (a decreasing number, thankfully) who get stuck into religion, who pile on religious behaviour and fulfil every religious duty scrupulously. The danger that lurks around such highly religious people was highlighted by Jesus and recorded in Matthew's Gospel chapter 23, namely, that religion can become a substitute for a relationship with the living God. Religion without relationship can as easily lead to the same fundamental insecurity in what is changeless, as can relationship without religion.

When we look at what can change, we find another division, this time between preservationists and conservationists. Preservationists seek to put history back into the bottle or the old oak tree back into the acorn; to reproduce the past as though it is happening now, the approach taken by Disney World re-creations. Some try to stop the passage of time, to arrest the clock of history: occasionally custodians of ancient monuments fall into this trap, carefully preserving ruins an attempt to stop the old oak tree growing and decaying. Conservationists, on the other hand, seek to make the best of the past in the present for the future: it is the approach taken by those who know that time and history are like a river, constantly on the move, aware that the present must make its contribution to the invaluable heritage of the past and leave room for new contributions in the future. This attempt respects the old oak, lops off branches where necessary, nurtures it, and creates good conditions for its future flourishing and, at the right time, lets it die.

Archbishop Alwyn Rice Jones pointed out that

'The very word "change" causes us discomfiture. The hymn has made us link the word 'change' with 'decay', whereas it can mean new beginning, new growth. Someone remarked that the structures of the church have the engine power of a lawn mower and the brakes of a juggernaut! Such is our instinctive and structural conservatism. But in times of whirlwind developments in communications and yet of galloping disintegration in society, we need to know the difference between the eternally significant in our heritage, and the merely evanescent.'[9]

Anything that grows changes. Resist change and growth stops. One of the tell-tale signs of this resistance is the classic excuse, 'We tried that and it didn't work!' The Apostle Paul anticipated change and growth in his volcanic Letter to the Romans. He spent what we call the first 11 chapters describing universal human sin and omnipotent divine grace, the infinite love of God for lost humanity and the free gift of a restored relationship with God by faith, the power of God to bring life out of death and his eternal purpose for all creation tasted in the promise of the Holy Spirit. Then, aware as Paul always was that the old is passing away and Christ is renewing creation, he turns at the beginning of chapter 12 from these magisterial truths to their application - the 'therefore' gives it away. All that he has taught about the mercies of God must now bear fruit in positive Christian discipleship and the willingness to be changed.

'Therefore, my friends, I implore you by God's mercy to offer your very selves to him: a living sacrifice, dedicated and fit for his acceptance, the worship offered by mind and heart. Conform no longer to the pattern of this present world, but be transformed by the renewal of your minds. Then you will be able to discern the will of God, and to know what is good, acceptable, and perfect.'[10]

Time, for Paul, was split into what he called 'this age' and 'the age to come', an age of rebellion and an age when everything is brought into subjection to God. This is not a chronological sequence of moments that can be measured with a clock, it is an existence, an opportunity within an eternity, God's moment. The Apostle writes elsewhere of disciples being those 'on whom the ends of the ages have come',[11] those who have the promise and assurance of the Spirit[12] as the light of dawn begins to appear over the horizon. Christians live at this connecting-point of the two 'ages', at the point at which the spark jumps between the two terminals, the ends of the almost-touching fingers of God and Adam which are, at least for me, the focus of Michelangelo's ceiling in the Sistine Chapel, Rome. As we've observed before, living at the end and the beginning of the two ages forces us to live with paradox, and paradoxes are never easy to live with!

Our environment tends to condition our responses to life, maybe not entirely, as the behaviourists would wish us to believe, for we are more than hungry rats in a maze. Yet if you live with violence you will tend to accept violence as normal and you might become violent; if you live dominated by money and possessions you will find it hard to understand why some people want to achieve international debt relief. Similarly, living too comfortably in this age leads us to behave as if we were not also citizens of the age to come. Christians live at the end and the beginning of the ages, which means we live by higher standards tomorrow than those of yesterday; the way of Christ is what Paul describes as 'the will of God, knowing what is good, acceptable and perfect'. If Christ calls us his friends, as he does, the way we live must reflect his moral, spiritual and divine beauty.

So Paul finds himself describing change in the Christian disciples of Rome as a process of continual change and growth towards the will of God. God's way is 'good', 'pleasing' and 'complete' - whole, not something partial which leaves more still to be achieved, the unblemished gift of being caught up in his will and doing as he wants.

So how is this to happen? By 'presenting your bodies as a living sacrifice, holy and acceptable to God'. Everything about yourself which can be offered, everything that is the gift of God, other than the tarnishing corrosion of sin, is to be offered to him, including the body, because the followers of the incarnate Word are not afraid of their bodies. It's a matter of being made holy – different in God's way.

Offer yourself 'as a living sacrifice', a marked contrast with the old cult of killing an animal as a sacrifice; not something done to earn favour with a reluctant god, but the self-offering of the redeemed to the Redeemer. In English the word 'lively' has changed its meaning since it was used in the earlier biblical translations, because it suggests to us today something rushing about. In some ways it's a pity we've lost the old description of the redeemed life offered to God as 'a lively sacrifice' with its sense of vitality and energy.

This 'living, holy and acceptable sacrifice' is 'the worship offered by mind and heart' - Paul uses the word from which we derive 'logical' to describe this true service Christians offer to God. It's a matter of engaging all our powers of reason in lives directed to pleasing God. Paul contrasts a total, spiritual offering of oneself with the cheap offering of convenient things, 'things which cost me nothing'.[13]

In this self-offering, 'Do not,' he writes, 'be conformed to the standards of this world' - that is, literally, 'to this age'. We must be conformed to the standards of the age to come. This applies equally to all who are Christian disciples - not simply to pastors, priests, church leaders or any particular group - but to us all, and in some of our church in-fighting as well as in our daily witness we do well to remember that. The change which Paul desires for disciples takes place by our being, in his words, 'transformed by the renewing of your minds'. This is an odd expression because the word 'transformation' (from the Greek word *metamorphosis*) means to change something's *external* form, its outward appearance; and we know that God looks on the heart for it is the heart that must change, a fact in which we rejoice but which can make Christian mission so annoyingly difficult. The last thing one would expect Paul to commend would be a change of external appearance and that's clearly not what he was trying to convey. What he's struggling to find words to describe is much deeper. The 'renewal of your minds' is a profound change of nature that involves repentance (a change of mind), a new way of thinking, the exchange of one's natural outlook for the mind of Christ.

'Transubstantiation' is a word used by Roman Catholics to describe a change in the essential nature of the bread and wine during the Mass. I would like to borrow that word to describe the process of change in the disciple's inner-most being, a complete renewal at the centre of all that we are and all that we will be.

Elsewhere St Paul writes of

'seeing the glory of the Lord with unveiled faces, as though reflected in a mirror, and being transformed into the same image from one degree of glory to another'.[14]

That change from the likeness of the old Adam and Eve to the likeness of Christ, from 'the image of the man of dust' to its fulfilment in 'the image of the man of heaven'[15] is radical, a transubstantiation going on in the lives of all disciples of Christ by the working of the Holy Spirit. There is no such thing as growth without change - in any sphere of life.

'In a higher world it is otherwise, but here below to live is to change, and to be perfect is to have changed often.'[16]

In some cases, the fear of the very idea of change is rooted in the comfort that being a Christian and belonging to the Church brings. This sense of comfort and belonging can become the over-riding reason for being a Christian: Sunday worship and the familiar, reassuring features of worship can become an escape from the busy-ness of life and from the speed of change in the contemporary world. On Easter Day in 1983, as the very new vicar of a large parish and in a full church, I encouraged the congregation to share the peace, and most people threw themselves into it. On the way out I was faced with a very angry parishioner who told me he came to church to worship God, not to be friendly with other people! While recognising the great importance of comfort in belonging in Christ, it can be difficult to lead some people out of a retreat-ism complex; whole congregations that get stuck into retreat-ism are a major cause of ministers throwing in the towel and younger disciples looking elsewhere for meaning and belonging.

On the other hand, worship in community should be a major formative influence on disciples; it shapes us from just thinking about how to love the stranger into people who are willing to be among those who are strangers, by inhabiting the places where we ourselves feel disempowered like new apprentices. Popular thinking today about personal relationships tells people that if they don't feel like staying together, or if they run into hard times, then they should just opt out – sometimes with dire consequences for the next generation. Worship is a space where people who would not otherwise have much in common can come together as strangers, and learn in the presence of God to live among and enjoy the company of people and situations they would otherwise find difficult. This apprenticeship integrates friendship with the formation of character, as it did for the disciples of Jesus and the early Church, though not without friction on occasions![17] It has been said that 'the plural of disciple is church'. The Church is the calling together of Jesus' apprentices, the formation of the people of God in common worship.

A more constructive side to the fear of change is the feeling that the heart of something may be lost in the process of changing it. C.S. Lewis put that fear neatly:

'change is not progress unless the core remains unchanged. A small oak grows into a big oak; if it became a beech, that would not be growth, but mere change.'[18]

Maturity, 'the capacity to endure uncertainty',[19] cannot develop if there remains insecurity about essentials. Thus, a relationship can endure many changes in the passage of time and can even face momentous upheavals, provided that its basis is sound. In terms of discipleship, this foundation is a matter of prioritising the relationship with God in Christ in the Spirit, and being secure but not self-confident in it.

In the Gospels Simon Peter is an intriguing character whose discipleship led him into apparently constant change, whether it was his weakness of faith, his blurting out the wrong thing, his failures of courage, his vacillations over whether gentiles could become Christians without first accepting the Hebrew faith, and so on. In all this, his confession of Jesus as the Christ, the Messiah, stands out[20] as a point of no return both for him and for the band of disciples. John, writing as most scholars believe, towards the close of the first century AD, builds this complexity of character into his picture of Peter.

At the beginning of the Gospel, Andrew brings his brother to Jesus. 'Simon, son of John,' Jesus calls him, 'you shall be called Cephas,' (a *double entendre* which John explains means 'Peter', 'the Rock').[21] There are strong connections between this early part of the Gospel and its conclusion, so when we turn to what looks like a symbolic post-script, we find that Jesus three times returns to using the same name:

'Jesus said to Simon Peter, "Simon son of John, do you love me more than these others?" "Yes, Lord," he answered, "you know that I love you." "Then feed my lambs," he said. A second time he asked, "Simon son of John, do you love me?" "Yes, Lord, you know I love you." "Then tend my sheep." A third time he said, "Simon son of John, do you love me?" Peter was hurt that he asked him a third time, "Do you love me?" "Lord," he said, "you know everything; you know I love you." Jesus said, "Then feed my sheep." '[22]

Peter had not been called 'Simon son of John' since Jesus called him at the beginning of the Gospel so it's intriguing to think why the name appears again at the end. By the time the Gospel was written Peter had become one of the two leading apostles of the Church and had died a martyr in Rome. Perhaps Jesus and the writer in this second passage were trying to get behind the public persona of Peter as a prominent leader to Peter as he was when they first met. In the words of Bishop Gordon Mursell,

'Jesus takes Peter back to before he became a disciple, as though to ask, "Are you really sure you want to go through with this? Which identity do you want to put first – Simon son of John or Peter the rock?" '[23]

Of course, the readers of the Fourth Gospel all knew the answer to Jesus' challenge to Peter - namely that he would indeed fulfil what Jesus had said –

' "When you are old you will stretch out your arms, and a stranger will bind you fast, and carry you where you have no wish to go." He said this to indicate the manner of death by which Peter was to glorify God. Then he added, "Follow me." '[24]

The question is now turned onto the reader. Which identity do you choose as a disciple? Your public identity or the unique person re-formed in the image of Christ? 'Follow me.'

In St Paul's most joyful letter, Philippians, he reminds his readers in that secular metropolis about his own discipleship, both in terms of where he came from, where he is, and where he hopes to be:

'I press on, hoping to take hold of that for which Christ once took hold of me.'[25]

Christ took hold of the world on the cross and in his resurrection: to that Paul clings more-and-more each day. But he was also personally aware that Christ took hold of him on the Damascus Road, at the moment when he heard Jesus speak to him and call him away from being a persecutor to be a disciple; and in time Saul (the name of the first warrior-king of Israel) became Paul (the little one). That moment of conversion could never be erased from Paul's life or spiritual awareness, the moment 'Christ once took hold of me'. If the Church is to endure change, it must find its security both in the great works of God in Christ, and also in those moments when Christ took hold of each one of us and we said 'Yes' to being his disciples.

But it's not all about us, of course. Being disciples makes us Christians at home, at work, in voluntary action, among people in crisis, at foodbanks, among homeless people, in politics, with young and old, caring for the environment, in the media, on holiday, in the arts and sciences, the list is endless because being disciples is for all of us simply living Christianly.

In 2014 my former diocese held its second ministry conference at which Professor Leslie Francis led three interesting Bible studies on discipleship, having first divided the participants into four groups according to an initial Myers Briggs personality test. [26] One study was based on a passage from Mark's Gospel in which Jesus sends out the twelve disciples two-by-two, and King Herod hears about it and thinks John the Baptist may have been raised from the dead.[27] If the correct translation of Mark's account is 'began to send them out'[28] – and the word 'began' is there in the Greek – then it seems clear that the disciples were not all sent out together but in pairs to practice, return, reflect with the community and be taught.

'As he went round the villages teaching, he summoned the Twelve and began to send them out two by two with authority over unclean spirits. He instructed them to take nothing for the journey except a stick - no bread, no pack, no money in their belts. They might wear sandals, but not a second coat. "When you enter a house," he told them, "stay there until you leave that district. At any place where they will not receive you or listen to you, shake the dust off your feet as you leave, as a solemn warning." So they set out and proclaimed the need for repentance; they drove out many demons, and anointed many sick people with oil and cured them.'

The dominant sensing, 'facts' people were comfortable with the idea of staying in places where they were made welcome but uncomfortable in places where they weren't. The 'solemn warning' to those who wouldn't listen was hard for them to accept. They took from the passage the need for team-working, travelling light, trusting God while knowing they had a secure base.

The dominant intuitive, 'big-ideas' group let it all hang out: here was Jesus removing his support from and simultaneously giving his authority to a partly-formed rag-bag of disciples. No wonder Herod mistook them for John the Baptist, so perhaps Christians should look more distinctive. Should we be looking for a niche in which we feel welcome or always be ready to move on?

The dominant feeling, 'relationships' folk were a bit scared at the thought of no bread, money or second pair of shoes, but the disciples had a new empowerment to overcome these fears. How did they cope with being empowered by Jesus without it going to their heads? The disciples had taken enormous risks, going out of their comfort zone and messing with demons.

The dominant thinking, 'theological' types saw the urgency of Jesus' commission but that he had given them very little instruction. They were not to waste time on unreceptive people; being in pairs gave them companionship and strengthened their credibility. We should not automatically expect people to want the gospel of forgiveness if they don't realise their need of it.

Four very different sets of reactions to Jesus' call of the first disciples from four groups of people, almost all of whom are preachers, reading the same, familiar text. One feature appears in the thinking of all, and that is the radically transformed nature of what Jesus expected of these early disciples, both as individuals and as a community.

It has become common to speak of 'Education For Discipleship'. Increasingly this is seen as an unhelpful term to describe the process and content of adult Christian transformation. There are essentially two complementary processes. 'Education' is the process of learning the skills necessary to understand and appropriate the beliefs, attitudes and values of a Christian disciple. But 'formation' is the parallel process by which a disciple's faith, attitudes, values, etc. are shaped into Christ-likeness. Both are integral to the on-going process of transforming discipleship.

The 'Great Commission' of Jesus recorded at the end of Matthew's Gospel provides a bird's-eye view of transforming discipleship:

'Jesus came near and said to them: "Full authority in heaven and on earth has been committed to me. Go therefore to all nations and make them my disciples; baptize them in the name of the Father and the Son and the Holy Spirit, and teach them to observe all that I have commanded you. I will be with you always, to the end of time." '[29]

This passage, like equivalent passages in Luke, Acts and John,[30] emphasises the transfer of authority and power of Christ himself, the gift of the Holy Spirit, to the disciples as the next wave of God's mission by the apostles, the sent-ones.

Apart from the command to 'Go!' three activities are specified, as has been noted earlier: make disciples, baptize and teach obedience to the Lord's commands. These have been the three indelible marks of the mission entrusted to the Christian Church ever since. The three marks have fluid edges and blend with one another. For 'making disciples' the word 'evangelism' will do, baptism is clear, and for 'teaching obedience' let's use the word 'formation'; none of these words do justice to what lies behind them but they are useful shorthand for the sake of understanding the process of transformation to which we are called.

Some churches work on a model of mission that starts with evangelism, moves to baptism and then on to formation. In this context, what triggers baptism is a response to evangelism, followed by nurture and formation. Often, in this context, baptism is reserved for those who are able to make a decision for Christ, that is, as adults.

Others work on a model for mission that starts with baptism and then blends evangelism with ongoing formation. In this context, baptism may take place any time after birth and the process of formation will be combined with evangelism, leading to a response, often formalised in a ceremony such as confirmation. This was the model operated by most of the Church in its various Christendom forms until relatively recent times, and 'catechesis', that is teaching people the ways of the Lord, was a more clearly-defined stage in the process in preparation for adult discipleship.

Increasingly, people come to faith less by a specific evangelistic approach than through the personal witness of a friend, possibly leading to a nurture group such as Alpha or Pilgrim. For the increasing number of people not baptized as children, baptism follows or, for those already baptized, there will normally be some public affirmation of faith. So catechesis takes place in a much greater variety of contexts than ever before but ultimately it is there to enable Christians to understand and apply the process of transformation into Christ-likeness which is at the heart of being a disciple.

It's not only individual disciples that experience change: churches, too, can change. The local church in Britain today is less aware of itself as a beach-head to the Kingdom of God than as a stretch of sand on the Costa Little. Churches, both as local communities and as denominations, need to change. Scott Peck returns to the idea that all life is process:

'All organisations are in process, but the healthier they are, the more they will be in process. The more vibrant, the more lively they are, the more they will be changing.'[31]

Although we believe that the motivating force behind change is the power of the Holy Spirit, the phases through which they change are similar to those experienced by any other organisation. In every church there will be advocates, uncommitted people and opponents of change. Advocates do not need to be convinced and may even need a little restraining. The uncommitted who think through the ideas will need to be helped and encouraged. Opponents are unlikely to be convinced and need simply to be identified and cared for. Across all there will be those who are anxious: time and effort needs to be spent with them – and they may be the majority.

When change is proposed there may be an initial burst of energy, followed by a range of emotions that can easily be passed from one person to another and there often comes a time, a pit of confusion, when the leader needs all his or her stamina to stay with a vision and see the positive developments grow, flower and bear fruit.

Those who, like me, have spent some time leading people through change know that the process is a complicated one. There are people who will tell you how to manage all forms of change. I am sceptical of that broad-brush approach but I do believe people can be led, often one at a time, to understand and cope constructively with the positive and negative influences on them. Pastors who want to see change happen should pay more attention to this one-to-one ministry among their people. Though it is possible to observe well-known patterns of behaviour, each individual will react differently to change. Self-awareness is a gift not many naturally possess, so wise leaders will take advice on whether they can do process; if not, they need the discernment and humility to find someone else gifted in the art of gracious and effective change.

I think of two of the initiatives in my former diocese on the Isle of Man. One is based in a village with an early 19th century church building that originally doubled as the local school. The folk there became committed to the principle that, in their own words, "we're here to serve the needs of the whole of our community, offering a central and easily accessible gathering point for everyone in the village. We encourage active community involvement in village concerns, social gatherings, and neighbourhood support and outreach." The success of that venture can be seen at www.stjamesdalby.org   Another initiative was in a large suburban parish with a church in one corner of the area and a reputation (which may or may not have been fair) of fund-raising for its buildings. A new vicar realised that it had some extensive grounds and so decided to offer a free bonfire and fireworks display on 5th November. Nearly 1,000 people turned up - and in subsequent years - and, as a result, greater numbers of people have turned to the church at special times in their lives. The church is seen as a generous giver.

The point of this is to say that the transformation of a disciple is fundamentally linked to the transformation of the church, and that it is facile and completely unrealistic to say that either can be achieved simply and without cost.

'Come, come,' wrote John Bunyan (1628-88), 'conversion is not so easy and so smooth a thing, as some would have men believe it is. Why is man's heart compared to fallow ground, God's Word to a plow, and his ministers to plowmen; if the heart indeed has no need of breaking in order to the receiving of the seed of God unto eternal life'.[32]

Transformation, 'the renewal of your minds', like the call of Christ, can be painful both for disciples and for churches.

'But why?' people ask. 'Why shouldn't the church stay as I knew it when I first joined and remain that way until I die?' Because the world is changing and God is waiting ahead of you to lead you into the future. And also because those who are unwilling to live as contemporary disciples are heard to proclaim an unintended message that Christ is for the past, not the present or the future. The man and woman in the street look at churches that are stuck in the past and ask why this faith has nothing to offer to the present day, let alone the future. Friedrich Nietzsche (1844-1900), the philosopher who expounded the 'God is dead' theory, is said to have observed,

'I might believe in the Redeemer if his followers looked more redeemed.'

Nietzsche's characteristic question must be taken seriously because he put his finger on a real weakness, a perceived failure by Christians to look like what they profess to be. Being redeemed (not just looking redeemed) is what is happening to you and me now as members of the body of Christ and agents of God's redemptive purposes. In a rapidly changing world, that means changing to keep up with God.

It is to that constantly renewed and renewing discipleship that Christ himself keeps calling us, and, through us, to the world: 'Come, follow me!'

Almighty God,
in Christ you make all things new:
transform the poverty of our nature by the riches of your grace,
and in the renewal of our lives
make known your heavenly glory;
through Jesus Christ your Son our Lord.
Amen.

(Collect of the 2nd Sunday of Epiphany)

References

1. One version of a much-quoted prayer referred to by V. Collancy: God of a Hundred Names.
2. M Scott Peck: A World Waiting to be Born.
3. Revelation 4. 8b; see also 1. 4, 8.
4. The journey begins at Luke 9. 51-53.
5. Mark 3. 31-35.
6. Matthew 8. 22; Luke 9. 57-62.
7. Mark 1. 14, 15.
8. Karl Barth and others.
9. 1994 Annual Review of the Board of Mission of Church in Wales.
10. Romans 12. 1, 2.
11. 1 Corinthians 10. 11.
12. 2 Corinthians 1. 22; 5. 5; Ephesians 1. 14.
13. 2 Samuel 24. 24.
14. 2 Corinthians 3. 18.
15. 1 Corinthians 15. 49.
16. John Henry (later Cardinal) Newman: Essay on the Development of Christian Doctrine, 1845.
17. Galatians 2. 1-14, particularly v 11.
18. Dogma and the Universe, 1943, in God in the Dock, Collins, 1979.
19. Professor John Finley.
20. Matthew 16. 16; Mark 8. 29; Luke 9. 20.
21. John 1. 42b.
22. John 21. 15-17.
23. Addresses on John 21, April 2015.
24. John 21. 18b, 19
25. Philippians 3. 12b.
26. See Rural Theology, vol 13.1, 2015, p 69ff.
27. Matthew 6. 6b-14.
28. Mark 6. 7.
29. Matthew 28. 18-20.
30. Luke 24. 47-51; Acts 1. 8; John 20. 21-23.
31. ibid.
32. The Acceptable Sacrifice or The Excellency of a Broken Heart, 1688.

7 Called to Serve

Over the years, churches have tried to focus on all kinds of activities in order to improve their techniques: praying more effectively (whatever that means), being better at witness, improving the quality of their service to the community, and so on. All worthy aims. During the last couple of generations, the buzz word has been 'ministry' and quite a trade was established in making Christians feel guilty if they weren't 'ministering', while fewer people outside wanted to join in this energetic activity. In contrast, my plea is to concentrate on helping Christians to be Christians by the power of the Holy Spirit, and allow church-based activity to run itself.

Service and servanthood are part of the DNA of every Christian disciple and of the Church.

'The Church exists to serve,' wrote Douglas Webster many years ago. 'It is only within this context that the Church's evangelism can be earthed and relevant and effective. Service to the world must be the unchanging background to the Church's witness. It is only the fulfilment of its role as a servant that entitles the Church to present Christ to the world it serves. The mere fact of availability to people, with no motive except to love and care for them, may have immense evangelistic significance in the long run ... The Church and the Christian alike are committed to service as the expression of the love and compassion of God in the name of Jesus Christ. Unless the Church is at home in the sphere of service, it is unlikely to be relevant when it turns to evangelism.'[1]

One of the obvious reasons for my passion for discipleship is that I fear too many experts have tried to take over the Church with their particular emphasis: evangelism, stewardship (using our gifts well), worship, ministry or whatever. Before long, everything gets eaten-up by one or other of these themes and, when that happens, the Church turns its gaze in on itself; we become bothered about ourselves above everything else, and the Church becomes the end, rather than the means. Instead of being concerned about what we ought to be concerned about - God and the world[2] - we become obsessed with Church.

The most all-consuming of these themes is 'ministry': the more our talk revolves around ministry, the more we devalue and disable Christian disciples whose calling is not to *do* something for the benefit of the church but to *be* Christians. Put simply, discipleship is what all Christians are called to – we are all disciples of the Lord – whereas ministry is a summons by the Lord to some activity and, in particular, an activity for and/or on behalf of the Church, normally related in some way to the sharing of the Word.

The concept of ministry has a range of interpreters. At one end of the scale are those who divide the Church into those who minister and those who don't; at the other end are those who assume that every Christian is a minister with at least one ministry. A couple of generations ago we were at one extreme and ministry normally meant ordination as a cleric. Then opinion swung to the other extreme, and ministry came to mean activities every Christian should engage in, calling each little act of service 'our ministry'. Both are fatal traps into which we easily fall. 'When all is ministry, ministry fades away.'[3] By becoming one of those token words that can be used for almost any Christian activity, ministry so easily - at least, in English - loses its root meaning of 'service'.

In the simplest and most basic sense, ministry describes our being servants of God - a calling for all Christians. But there is more to be said about this word and, in order to make sense of the New Testament and of God's work in today's world, we need to make clearer the distinctions between the service offered by all Christian disciples and commissioned ministry.

Let's not under-estimate the power of sacrificial service. You often have to look hard to discover service because true servants don't boast about it. Take Andrea, for example, the manager of a rural community café started by church members but now run (on ethical principles) by volunteers from the whole community for the benefit of the whole community. And Helen, leading the 'Kitchen for Everyone', again started by Christians and serving meals to homeless people and those in need on a couple of days each week. Examples like this - foodbanks, Street Angels and Street Pastors, homeless shelters, and so much more, founded in Christian love - can be found in every city and town, and in many smaller communities as well.

It's worth taking a look at how the Church's understanding of ministry (or 'diakonia' in the Greek of the New Testament) has shifted in recent years. From early times, the concept was reasonably understood as a servant's commission from a superior body; that understanding remained unchallenged at the Reformation, until the twentieth century. The monumental change occurred between the Third ecumenical World Conference on Faith and Order held at Lund in 1952 and the Fourth Conference at Montreal in 1963, a change that has affected Christian thinking ever since.

In 1952 the traditional assumption was that ministry was provided (in the words of St Paul) by God 'to equip the saints';[4] but, by 1963, there was an unequivocal (and I would add, speculative) assertion that ministry is the prerogative of all the baptized. This is the first point at which the representatives of the mainstream churches worldwide linked ministry directly with baptism, the call to be a disciple: 'every-member ministry' was well and truly launched! Though he was, in some respects merely collating what a small number of theologians had come to assert during the period since the 1930's, perhaps the most influential exponent of this new thinking was Hendrik Kraemer,[5] the first director of the World Council of Churches' Study Centre.

The *'Baptism, Eucharist and Ministry'* (Lima) report of the World Council of Churches in 1982 placed a valuable emphasis on the part played by every Christian in the mission of God, but there was also some blurring when, for example, it declared:

'The word ministry in its broadest sense denotes the service to which the whole people of God is called'.

This thinking further encouraged many to declare that baptism was a universal sign of gifting for ministry, that 'every-member ministry' or 'the ministry of the baptized' was a given, a New Testament doctrine, and that the terms 'discipleship' and 'lay ministry' meant the same thing. The natural corollary of this was that all Christians should seek out their own ministry.

So 'ministry' became a word that found its way into every thought for the renewal of the Church's life: in one commentator's words, 'Ministry is a greedy concept.'[6] This thinking became the touchstone of strategies for mission and ministry and still remains stubbornly embedded. The failure to distinguish the two ways in which we understand the word *'diakonia'* as (1) the service offered by every disciple and (2) the ministry to which some have been committed has led to confusion in our thinking about ministry, particularly lay ministry, and devalued the discipleship shared by all Christians. Ray Anderson commented that

'mission keeps ministry from becoming a mirror in which the church, like the mythical Narcissus, sees its own reflection and ends up withering away until it becomes a potted plant - a narcissus!'[7]

As well as becoming a word that finds its way into every thought for the renewal of the Church's life, ministry has also acquired, in many church-people's hearing, the sense that it is to do with service within the Church or on behalf of the Church, that it is, deep down, Church ministry. Thus the nagging questions which hang around in some churches, 'What's your ministry? What are you doing for the Church?' This persistent emphasis on every disciple being a minister shifts the focus of attention subconsciously from Christian discipleship to a preoccupation with 'ministries'. It's not that all of these are unnecessary or under-valued, because sustaining the life of the Church is vital, but the emphasis has shifted.

The Church today, it is said, is like a helicopter: don't stand too close or you may get sucked into its rotas! Take a look at some of the notice boards in churches and church halls: you'll find ministries for welcoming, hospitality, refreshments, prayer, worship, music, children, youth, healing, and goodness knows what else! - all this ministering while fewer people out there in society want to belong. Whether such ministries are accredited or not, we have witnessed a gradual clericalising of lay people, diverting attention from the kingdom of God and the world he loves into internal affairs.

John N. Collins, who has led much of the renewed study of the word since the early 1970's,[8] and others, have looked at how the various *'diakon-'* words were used within the first century world of the New Testament writers, and recognised that, while they did carry some overtones of humility, they primarily describe honourable, commissioned service. His work has been an important driver behind recognising a distinction between the servanthood of all baptized Christians and the ministry of those (lay and ordained) to whom has been committed commissioned and reserved service. In other words, we need to retreat from the language of 'every-member ministry' and replace it with 'every disciple a servant'.

Collins's research into the use that classical writers (secular and religious) of the New Testament period made of the ministry/service words, and the divergent understandings that have prevailed for half a century may be summarised in the following way:[9]

Ministry as commonly understood		*According to Greek literary sources*
An ordinary, everyday word	$\longrightarrow$	A word with literary and poetic quality
A religious-neutral term	$\longrightarrow$	Commonly used in religious contexts
Originally, 'service at table'	$\longrightarrow$	Service at table is only one application
Used of slaves	$\longrightarrow$	Customarily an honourable designation
Used by Christians because it suggested lowliness	$\longrightarrow$	Used as appropriate language for exercising functions in a community

Ministry is lowly service	→	Ministry is high office
Adapted by Christians to express loving service of one another	→	Not an expression of loving service, but of executing a mandate from a superior
Ministry is for all	→	Ministry is a reserved function

Collins concludes that at no point in ancient usage, Christian, pagan or secular, did ministry mean loving service to those in need. The overwhelming majority of New Testament scholarship now supports this understanding of ministry as commissioned and accountable service. So let's see what three important texts in the New Testament can teach us.

First, one of Jesus' sayings from Matthew's and Mark's Gospels:

'The Son of Man did not come to be served but to serve, and to give his life as a ransom for many.'[10]

The background of the saying is the request of his disciples James and John to sit next to Jesus at his throne in the Kingdom (Matthew says it was their mother who asked). As we noted in chapter 5, Jesus begins by explaining,

' "You do not understand what you are asking. Can you drink the cup that I drink, or be baptized with the baptism I am baptized with?" "We can," they answered. Jesus said, "The cup that I drink you shall drink, and the baptism I am baptized with shall be your baptism; but to sit on my right or on my left is not for me to grant; that honour is for those to whom it has already been assigned." '[11]

The description of this situation provides the backdrop for the saying which follows it: that a disciple must be humble and ready to follow Jesus into the baptism of suffering. The saying itself, like the story in which it is set, is in two parts that are inextricably linked by a crucial 'and'. Yes, 'the Son of Man came not to be served but to serve' - and here a comma gets in the way, with the danger that we might take the rest of the sentence for granted - 'and to give his life as a ransom for many.' In other words, the service offered by the Son of Man is not so much his humility *per se*, but his giving his life as a ransom for many - 'the baptism I am baptized with'. He is a humble servant because he is an obedient servant.

Undoubtedly, a contrast in status between the One being served and the Servant is part of the intention of the Evangelists; but we have so emphasised the humility of Jesus that we have missed the greater point: the commissioned service of the Son who lays down his life for humanity at the behest of the Father. This is basic to understanding the incarnation and mission of Jesus, that his service, his earthly ministry was as the Servant commissioned by the Father for the benefit of many. John Collins comments:

'Mark's Son of Man is serving or, better, ministering under God. In laying down his life, he is carrying out the sacred commission or *diakonia* he had received from God.'[12]

Those who have attended church services on Maundy Thursday may have experienced a foot-washing ceremony in which the presiding minister (representing Jesus) symbolically washes the feet of some members of the congregation to illustrate the reading of John's Gospel chapter 13.

'Jesus 'rose from the supper table, took off his outer garment and, taking a towel, tied it round him. Then he poured water into a basin, and began to wash his disciples' feet and to wipe them with the towel. ...
[v.12] After washing their feet he put on his garment and sat down again. "Do you understand what I have done for you?" he asked. "You call me Teacher and Lord, and rightly so, for that is what I am. Then if I, your Lord and Teacher, have washed your feet, you also ought to wash one another's feet. I have set you an example: you are to do as I have done for you. In very truth I tell you, a servant is not greater than his master, nor a messenger than the one who sent him. If you know this, happy are you if you act upon it." '[13]

In itself that is powerful liturgical theatre, but the choice of actors changes our perception of the reading. What happens is that the humble servanthood of Christ in the foot-washing image overtakes and restricts the meaning of the symbol when it is acted by a minister. It helps to read that part of the story that is sometimes omitted between verses 5 and 12 above:

'When he came to Simon Peter, Peter said to him, "You, Lord, washing my feet?" Jesus replied, "You do not understand now what I am doing, but one day you will." Peter said, "I will never let you wash my feet." "If I do not wash you," Jesus replied, "you have no part with me." "Then, Lord," said Simon Peter, "not my feet only; wash my hands and head as well!" Jesus said to him, "Anyone who has bathed needs no further washing; he is clean all over; and you are clean, though not every one of you." He added the words "not every one of you" because he knew who was going to betray him.'[14]

Peter's willingness to follow Jesus into his baptism of suffering is the key that unlocks the foot-washing symbol. Jesus is the Servant of God not simply because he is humble but because he is the Son obedient to the commission of his Father, his baptism of suffering, the commission that led to the cross.

This linking of Jesus' self-emptying with his obedience to the Father's commission is at the heart of the poem quoted by St Paul in his Letter to the Philippians to which we have referred before:

'Take to heart among yourselves what you find in Christ Jesus: He was in the form of God; yet he laid no claim to equality with God, but made himself nothing, assuming the form of a slave. Bearing the human likeness, sharing the human lot, he humbled himself, and was obedient, even to the point of death, death on a cross! Therefore God raised him to the heights and bestowed on him the name above all names, that at the name of Jesus every knee should bow—in heaven, on earth, and in the depths - and every tongue acclaim, "Jesus Christ is Lord," to the glory of God the Father.'[15]

The second passage for reflection is from St Paul's Second Letter to the Corinthians, the same letter in which the Apostle has been at pains to emphasise the link between his personal weakness and his role as an apostle, summed up in describing himself as a 'minister of Christ'.[16] Secular usage in ancient classical literature and from the first century in particular provides ample evidence that this word we translate as 'minister/servant' was also commonly used for a 'messenger' or, more to the point, an 'envoy', 'ambassador' or 'go-between'.

St Paul engages in a wide-ranging discussion of ministry extending over several chapters of 2 Corinthians.[17] One of the potential traps in this passage is that Paul consistently uses what is for us the archaic first person plural, 'we', when in normal English usage we would use the singular, 'I'. This use can still be heard in particularly formal political, legal or ecclesiastical documents, as in 'We, Robert, by divine permission Lord Bishop of Sodor and Man'. The trap is that it's very easy to assume Paul meant all of us when he was simply writing about himself.

As a servant/minister, he sees himself as the envoy sent from God with a word from God himself, not simply as a representative of the church in Jerusalem or Antioch. This divine commission is emphasised in the three accounts in The Acts of the immediate aftermath of his conversion.[18] Paul came to Corinth as God's envoy to bring his word of reconciliation in Christ;[19] his appeal was directly from God, and each time he uses that same word of himself - 'minister'. Important as it is to welcome people to worship or serve coffee afterwards, St Paul's use of the word 'minister' endows it with far greater significance than a 'welcoming ministry' or 'refreshment ministry' implies. As an apostle, Paul is a representative of the church that sent him and carries with him its credentials; as a minister, he is the spokesperson for God himself.

There is a possible significant exception when Paul writes, 'As an apostle to the Gentiles, I make much of [glory in] that ministry.'[20]   Yet it seems clear from the context - and most English translations make this clear - that his use of *diaconian* (ministry) here could as easily be translated as 'work' or 'what I have to do'.

The third observation is drawn from the Letter to the Ephesians.   What a difference a comma can make! If only Saint Paul's letters had punctuation. When the major updating of the popular Revised Standard Version of the Bible took place during 1971-2 a comma was omitted from the Letter to the Ephesians, chapter 4, verse 12.   Formerly it had read, 'for the equipment of the saints, for the work of ministry,' – referring to two distinct aspects of the effects of the ascended Christ's gifts to the Church - but it was revised in order to read, 'to equip the saints for the work of ministry.'

Without punctuation in the original or early texts we have no direct evidence to indicate what is the correct version; so we have to look elsewhere to understand what the original author intended.   What, for instance, may have influenced the revised translation without any textual evidence for either version?   The hidden persuader behind this change in the RSV seems clear to me, the growing popularity of every-member ministry in the 1960's and 70's (described above), itself an attempt at theological democracy, an understandable rebellion against a foolish hierarchical view of public ministry that put ordination at the top and discipleship at the bottom. Following the RSV revision, the comma separating the phrases was omitted from most other modern translations, including the Good News Bible, the New International Version, the New Jerusalem Bible, the Revised English Bible, and the New Revised Standard Version, thus linking the two concepts into one as in 'to prepare all God's people for the work of Christian service'.[21] Reading the revised text frequently in public worship has encouraged the popular view that apostles, prophets, evangelists, pastors and teachers are given to the Church in order to make all disciples into ministers. The scholarship to which I have referred above, in which ministry is commissioned and accountable service, makes it clear that St Paul must have seen the equipping of the saints as one activity, and the work of ministry as another. Earlier in Ephesians[22] Paul had defined this work of ministry as revealing the secret of the gospel, 'the good news of the unfathomable riches of Christ'.

The missing comma – such a small alteration – has dominated thinking about ministry and mission and has led to the false assumption that all the people of God are gifted for ministry. It has affected our perception of the role of the Church's public ministers: we have indoctrinated a couple of generations of clergy to think that their job is to turn entire congregations into ministry teams. 'Every-member ministry' has elbowed-out discipleship; the multiplication of ministries has displaced simply being Christian.

Ministry is about having a commission to fulfil. If my wife asks me to do an errand - let's say, to pick up some milk from a shop - I agree because my wife is the boss and I am the servant; my role in the errand is to serve someone else and to do it willingly. There's more. The errand itself matters because I have been commissioned to buy milk (rather than cheese) and bring it home. I am not only a servant but, more importantly, I am a commissioned and accountable envoy with a task to complete. It is this emphasis on being a commissioned agent - what in other contexts in the New Testament is sometimes called an ambassador - that we need to recover in our use of the word 'minister'. Confusing ministry with discipleship is not simply an arcane difference of opinion over words but a serious issue affecting the way the church operates.

It's necessary to add as an aside that most churches use the title 'deacon' to describe a ministerial office. The title is used in a wide range of ways across the churches, and this, in itself, reveals the confusion as to its origins. Yes, of course, these 'diakon-' words are fundamental to understanding the diaconate but the concept extends well beyond a specific order of ministry and sheds light on all areas of ministry in the Church, the whole range of called, selected, trained, commissioned and accountable public ministries, lay and ordained. So we have to loosen the ties between diakonia and the particular ministry of a deacon to allow its broader application. But this is not the place to discuss the diaconate in detail, fascinating though that may be for some.

As long ago as 1963, Kathleen Bliss pointed to the danger when 'jobs' become 'offices', when we fool ourselves into thinking that training for jobs in church means fulfilling a lay vocation.

'For what the laity lack is not the know-how of successful magazine distribution, but basic equipment in understanding what it means to be a Christian.'[23]

I'm convinced that the reason so few teenagers and younger adults want anything to do with us is not post-modernism, nor secularism, not scientific rationalism, nor any other of the alienating -isms, the power of which I do not deny: they don't think the church is any use! Christ has become absorbed by church. Why does this continue to happen? Because what's on the label is not what's in the tin. On the label it says, 'The Church - open here for salvation, peace, hope, purpose, love, healing & justice'; (it might also carry the caution 'This may contain nuts', and the sell-by date is fast approaching in some cases). Yet when the tin is opened, inside we find humbugs! People are not fooled. The Church that makes mighty claims for itself but doesn't deliver is in big trouble; worse still if it delivers a profoundly self-centred and self-satisfying ethic.   People outside the church have noticed this internalising tendency and don't want to belong to such an apparently useless and self-orientated organisation. We're not living the message that Church is good for God and the world, as well as for you.

Symptoms of this can be seen in the general decline of the self-preserving, self-absorbed parts of the institutional Church and the growth of the more visionary and less defensive. I see the same symptoms everywhere in declining churches: the internalising of energy, ministry displacing discipleship. It's easy to see how this internalisation happens. When every disciple is urged to be doing something (and every congregation has so many jobs to fill!), the church itself becomes the aim and thinking becomes subtly internalised. Even evangelism evolves into an activity the church engages in simply to bring more people in, to make 'my church' grow - sometimes, with more than a hint of desperation, so that my church will survive! - rather than the outward sharing of the priceless good news in Christ for the benefit of all. It's been parodied as,

'God so loved the Church that he gave his only Son, so that whoever believes in him may come to church and minister collaboratively'.

Ministry is always the servant of mission.   Ministry for its own sake is entertainment - keeping the troops contented until the day when we're all pushing-up daisies and the key in the church door is turned for the last time. Good, called, well-trained, accredited, commissioned and accountable ministers in many areas of witness are vital to equip the Church for the mission of God. Despite the few who scorn the use of that word 'mission', it is where God starts and ends. The very first Word uttered in the Bible, 'Let there be light!'[24] is where the record of God's mission began; it found its incarnation in Christ and the Church;[25] and that same mission finds fulfilment in the promised city of God: 'Come, Lord Jesus!'[26] It has been frequently well-said that,

'It is not the Church of God that has a mission to the world, but the God of mission who has a Church in the world.'[27]

However, let's not blur the distinctions between ministry and mission to such an extent that both become meaningless concepts. Mission, as we know, is very much a New Testament concept but not a New Testament word; ministry is both. There is a danger that the relationship between these two vital activities can be mis-read, confused and the proper distinctions between them not properly maintained.

All I have written before is in no way intended to suggest that commissioned ministers can forget the need for foot-washing humility. Church leaders, particularly those higher up the greasy pole, must lay aside a remote 'chief executive' style in favour of no less effective models of leadership; they will become leader-seekers on a common journey, not knowing the whole route ahead but with a contagious passion for the destination, humanity's true home in God. They must be people who can call others alongside in a common search for love, courage, wisdom, hope and life. That's the way of the Master.

All Christians are disciples of Christ by baptism and by accepting his call to 'Follow me' in faith. Discipleship does not discriminate between the followers of Jesus Christ, in terms of age, gender, ordination or ministry: there is no hierarchy among disciples. Everyday customs in the church may speak of this: Anglicans, for instance, will have come across the discipleship principle in such practices as the Prayer Book instruction for the minister to place the consecrated bread and wine *into the hands* of each person at the most sacred moment of Communion. It is nothing to do with any particular church tradition, it acts out an aspect of the Christian doctrine of discipleship, that there are no distinctions when the family of Christ gathers around his table.[28]

People embody the gospel. Jesus never wrote a book or established a school - we don't even recall his teachings in the creeds - because his greatest legacy is a community of people who live, not for the sake of that community, but for the sake of the good news that the community embodies.[29] In the secular sphere of expanding public institutions and growing individual self-interest, the church is often the only community-builder left. But sadly, by substituting ministry for discipleship, so many churches have themselves become like those public institutions, sucking people out of involvement with their neighbours (extracting the salt and covering the light) into endless activities which keep the institution going and keep disciples away from the world God loves. The hour or two people spend in worship each week with the Church is extremely important, but so is the way in which all the remaining hours of the week are spent. If all a disciple's precious hours of service are spent on propping-up the Church they are mis-spent, however important the Church is to God and us - and it is.

Being a disciple is about being a Christian, a servant of God, all the time and in every place. Christian witness in Britain today will not rely on campaigns but on this vital witness to Christ in his disciples, his exploded body whose presence, attitudes and actions raise such questions that others search for meaning in their lives. I am convinced that the equipping of disciples for Christian witness and service in all the places to which God calls us as human beings is more important to God's mission than strategies for ministry, since every disciple is a servant.

Two generations ago the Roman Catholic Church recognised that the Church itself and its ministry had become the defining model of its life. The Second Vatican Council (1962-5) sought to re-focus mission first on the kingdom of God, then on the proclamation of the gospel in the world, after that, on the Church, and finally, on the Church's ministry. In other words, the Council asserted that church is more important than ministry, gospel more important than church, kingdom more important than gospel and God most important of all. Those are wise priorities.

The role of the Church as the place where disciples are fed, nurtured and equipped should not be minimised if we are willing to be surprised by God at work among us. And, if we are to reverse the general decline of the self-preserving parts of the institutional Church, we need clarity of vision and some risk-taking. In practice that will be established by building strong foundations for Christian discipleship and by maintaining high expectations of those called to public ministry.

I am saddened that so many of the faithful are left unsure whether their discipleship has any value because it is not recognised for the wonderful thing it is: being Christian. If only we were less conscious of ministry, status and hierarchy and more conscious that we are all disciples, we might begin to think more clearly and serve more effectively.

Lord Jesus Christ,
you humbled yourself in taking the form of a servant,
and in obedience died on the cross for our salvation:
give us the mind to follow you
and to proclaim you as Lord and King,
to the glory of God the Father.
Amen.

(A prayer for use in Lent)

References

1. Douglas Webster: What is Evangelism?, (1959).
2. Leviticus 19. 18; Deuteronomy 6. 4; Matthew 22. 37; Mark 12. 30; Luke 10. 27.
3. T.F. O'Meara: Theology of Ministry, Paulist Press, 1983.
4. Ephesians 4. 12.
5. A Theology of the Laity, 1958.
6. Helen Oppenheimer.
7. Ray S Anderson: An Emergent Theology for Emerging Churches, B.R.F., 2007.
8. Diakonia: Re-interpreting the Ancient Sources, 1990; Are All Christians Ministers? 1992; etc.
9. ibid.
10. Matthew 20. 28; Mark 10. 45; see also Luke 22. 27, 28.
11. Mark 10. 38-40.
12. Journal of Ecumenical Studies, 1995
13. John 13. 4, 5, 12-15
14. John 13. 6-11.
15. Philippians 2. 5-11.
16. See 2 Corinthians 11. 23.
17. 2 Corinthians 2. 14 – 6.13.
18. See Acts 9. 15; 22. 14; 26. 16.
19. 2 Corinthians. 3. 8, 9; 5. 18
20. Romans 11. 13b.
21. Good News Bible. See also the Contemporary English version, 1995: 'so that his people would learn to serve and his body would grow strong'.
22. Ephesians 3. 1-13
23. We the People, SCM, 1963.
24. Genesis 1. 3.
25. John 20. 21.
26. Revelation 22. 20b.
27. Mission-Shaped Church report, 2004.
28. Galatians 3. 26-29.
29. Frequently said by Bishop Lesslie Newbigin – see The Gospel in a Pluralist Society, 1990, and The Open Secret, 1995.

8 Called to Grow

There is a Chinese proverb that says,

'Do not be afraid of growing slowly, simply be afraid of not growing at all.'

The Bible uses images of growth in describing the growth and development of individuals and communities in their relationship with God. We find the example of people such as Samuel and Jesus himself whose relationship with God developed as they grew;[1] illustrations of people as plants growing, flourishing and dying;[2] and most of chapter 13 of Matthew's Gospel is about living organisms – seeds, weeds, plants and yeast.[3] The powerful image of a child's growth from infancy pervades the New Testament letters,[4] as does the concept of the growth of a body to maturity.[5] So growth, particularly growth in our relationships with God and one another, was a priority for the authors of the Scriptures. Disciples have always been committed to a personal agenda of growth and, more than for many centuries, need to be committed to the Church's agenda for growth.

In a famous passage from John's Gospel Jesus told his disciples that because they – we - remain in the vine we will bear fruit that will last. As has been noted before, it raises the question of what being a disciple is for, what the Church is for, if not to produce results. Discipleship involves growth but how would we measure growth? Two millennia of studying the Scriptures have made it clear to us that these results, the fruit of growth are not to be measured from a secular or material viewpoint, but in the perspective of eternity with love at its focal point.

'This is how my Father is glorified: you are to bear fruit in plenty and so be my disciples. As the Father has loved me, so I have loved you. Dwell in my love. If you heed my commands, you will dwell in my love, as I have heeded my Father's commands and dwell in his love. ... You did not choose me: I chose you. I appointed you to go on and bear fruit, fruit that will last; so that the Father may give you whatever you ask in my name. This is my commandment to you: love one another.'[6]

Dwelling in the love of Christ is far more than making myself comfortable in my own spiritual nest. It is dwelling in the community of Christ, breaking bread and praying, living in the power of the Holy Spirit for the sake of the kingdom of God.[7] It is such a dwelling in the Centre of all things that through us the world itself may be transformed through us in justice and peace, just as the prophets of the Old Testament had proclaimed.

Some years ago, when the diocese of which I was bishop had developed its strap-line 'Together making Christ visible', I was asked whether I could define some areas of growth on which we could concentrate. So what follows reflects on those growth aims.

We pray for growth in ...
* spiritual life,
* understanding and practice,
* world awareness,
* youthfulness,
* ecumenical collaboration and
* numbers.

Spiritual life

Spirituality is popular these days, perhaps as an innate reaction to the scientism that restricts our thought and experience to what can be measured, or to the secularism that restricts our explanation of what can be true. Look in any bookshop at the large 'Body, Mind & Spirit' section and, among the shelves of books offering you advice on any number of spiritualities and alternative therapies, you may find a couple of presentation King James Bibles (for a bride or a confirmation candidate) and a Book of Common Prayer, but rarely anything else that is Christian. Down the street you will come across a shop that sells all the gear you need for spiritual exploits of every kind, and probably tickets for ghost-hunts. Around Hallowe'en, the shops will be drowning in ghoulish gear, to the delight of shopkeepers and spiritualists alike.

The danger with much practice of spirituality is that is purely about satisfying my own needs.

'You're a narcissist.' 'No I'm not,' came the angry reply from someone gazing rapturously in a mirror. 'A narcissist is someone who has a foolish infatuation with himself, but this is the real thing.'[8]

Looking into your soul is a very important Christian practice but it can also be a self-centred exercise, an indulgent attempt at do-it-yourself spiritual repair. Bishop Lesslie Newbigin described

'the narcissism which is so prevalent in our culture, the mentality which is interested only in its own selfhood and not in the realities of a world beyond the self. ... The name "Jesus" does not designate a plastic idea which can be moulded to suit my experience.'⁹

There is a very understandable tendency to make activist people like me - a colleague used to call me 'the Duracell bunny' - feel uncomfortable simply because we find the external world more in-Spiriting than the interior world favoured by many today. I'm hesitant about putting Christian disciples into spiritual compartments: the monastic community box (lots of contemplation), the evangelical box (lots of enthusiasm), the charismatic box (lots of feeling), and so on, because being in the wrong place can damage rather than repair our relationship with God. Somehow we have to embrace the immense variety of our God-given personalities and encourage a diversity of ways for all to access the renewing power of the Holy Spirit.

Contemporary disciples need to reclaim the spiritual world for Christ and to mark that world with the cross. Why the cross? Because the cross is the universal symbol of Jesus Christ, the Son of God, the Master, the Saviour, the Lord, to whom we believe all life owes its existence. And because it was his death on the cross that achieved what other spiritualities seek to achieve: forgiveness and reconciliation with God. There is no technique to be learned in order to receive the life of the Spirit, simply the acceptance of what God has done for us in Christ. That was Martin Luther's struggle as he studied the Letters to the Romans and Galatians in the second decade of the sixteenth century: how could he achieve forgiveness and reconciliation? In Christ. When John and Charles Wesley, methodical churchmen to their eighteenth century finger-tips, wrestled with how to make God appear less remote they found the answer in Christ.

Although those disciples who carry Christ on their shirt-sleeves can be a little off-putting, the unwillingness of many Christians to open up or even join a conversation about their spiritual life reveals an embarrassment about faith, or that for them church has replaced Christ.

Though in one sense the presence of the Holy Spirit remains undiminished in the life of the disciple, whatever life brings, there is also a very real sense in which his life grows within and among us. In the Second Letter of Peter we are urged to

'grow in grace and in the knowledge of our Lord and Saviour Jesus Christ,'¹⁰

what St Paul calls attaining to

'our knowledge of the Son of God, to mature manhood, measured by nothing less than the full stature of Christ. ... fully growing up into Christ,' ... 'a mature member of Christ's body.'¹¹

So our relationship with God in Christ, enabled by the Spirit, our 'faith, hope and love',[12] constantly need to be enriched, as in any other relationship, and to extend into every part of our lives so that there is no spiritual or religious compartment separated from what might be deemed secular or profane. Like any relationship, the relationship with God thrives on presence, which is another way of describing prayer and worship. I am haunted by a well-known saying of the young Scottish divine, Robert Murray McCheyne (1813-43) which convinces me that my life and my prayer must so seep into one another that ultimately they become one:

'What a man is on his knees before God, that he is and nothing more.'

The relationship with God is fed by prayer, scripture and sacrament. Prayer cannot really be described because words fall short. We have to rely on concepts with which we are more familiar in other settings: words like 'communion', 'intercourse' (in the sense of 'moving between') and 'breathing-space'. For me, no one has come closer to capturing the elusive ethos of prayer than George Herbert[13] in his poem 'Prayer (1)'.

'Prayer the Church's banquet, Angels' age,
God's breath in man returning to his birth,
The soul in paraphrase, heart in pilgrimage,
The Christian plummet sounding heav'n and earth;
Engine against th' Almighty, sinners' tower,
Reversed thunder, Christ-side-piercing spear,
The six-days world-transposing in an hour,
A kind of tune, which all things hear and fear;
Softness, and peace, and joy, and love, and bliss,
Exalted Manna, gladness of the best,
Heaven in ordinary, man well dressed,
The milky way, the bird of Paradise,
Church-bells beyond the stars heard, the soul's blood
The land of spices; something understood.'

Older Christians like me easily become victims of our own ambitions in prayer, judging ourselves by looking back to the days when it seemed so easy to pray, when words gushed out and feelings ran high. But in real relationships (human and divine) those times mature into something gentler. In settling down the wise Christian needs a simple basic framework for prayer and Bible reading - what clergy and those in religious orders call an 'office' - a disciplined time or times in every day when we approach our loving God through a blend of Scripture, praise, penitence, conversation, formality and spontaneity, under the guidance of the Holy Spirit. An example is provided in chapter 11. It's not we who do something for God but God who does something in us.

That personal experience of communion with God flows naturally into the gathering of the faithful week-by-week in worship, in which the sacraments are bound to feature prominently. Public worship is a habit that needs to be maintained. It's easy to slip out of worship – the kids have sport on Sunday morning, it's valuable family time, I need the rest (and God said resting once a week is a good idea). If the habit lapses, it's quite difficult to pick up again but well worth the effort.

St Augustine the African (354-430) likened the Bible to 'a letter sent from God',[14] a love-letter that reveals the sender; to be treasured and re-read; and, if we find it tiresome, we learn something serious about the quality of our love. If we rely on the extracts read in church on Sundays we are likely always to find the Bible confusing; the only way to get into it is to use some kind of consistent approach by which we follow the stories or teachings in their entirety.

I am cautious of what is sometimes called 'spiritual direction' because I doubt that the life of the Spirit in a disciple should always need to be 'directed'. I appreciate why a great many people feel the need for another disciple to reflect on their walk with Christ through life, so I prefer to speak of 'spiritual accompaniment' – always to be encouraged, though it may not be for all.

Spirituality begins and ends at the cross. There is no more. Taking his readers in Colossae back to their baptism and on to its fulfilment, St Paul wrote,

'For you were buried with him in baptism, and in that baptism you were also raised to life with him through your faith in the active power of God, who raised him from the dead. And although you were dead because of your sins and your uncircumcision, he has brought you to life with Christ. For he has forgiven us all our sins; he has cancelled the bond which was outstanding against us with its legal demands; he has set it aside, nailing it to the cross. There he disarmed the cosmic powers and authorities and made a public spectacle of them, leading them as captives in his triumphal procession.'[15]

It is in Christ that the life of the Spirit comes to us for it is in Christ that we are forgiven and reconciled. In him we receive the gift of the Spirit who brings Christ to us and bestows on us all the riches of his grace.

Understanding and practice

Why can't the pastor get her people along to a home group, or to regard worship as the top priority, or to see mission in its broadest terms, or to want to share the gospel? They'll tell her if she asks the right questions - they're not interested in the thing they call 'theology'! But, unless there's an attack of dry rot or death-watch beetle, just watch what happens if anyone suggests moving some pews out of the church building: the theologians appear out of the woodwork as if by magic, all keen to lecture her in a whole library's worth of systematic folk-theology!

And why is the church council so divided between people obsessed with gutters and downspouts, others inspired by pie in the sky, and passionate students of ecclesiastical law? Because their grasp of the breadth of Christian truth and practice is so limited. They suffer from an ecclesiastical bicycle shed mentality, like the board of directors of a multinational company that passes a £5-million advertising campaign on the nod because they've been advised to do it by their accountants and persuaded by communication experts, though they don't really understand it; but ask them to spend £2,000 on a bicycle shed and, even worse, ask them where it should be sited, and you could be in for a five-hour debate! They don't understand the big, costly issues, but they can talk about are trivial ones. What's worse is that they don't realise that they have a problem. The parallel with church is obvious.

The writer of the Letter to the Hebrews confronted a similar problem:

'By this time you ought to be teachers, but instead you need someone to teach you the ABC of God's oracles over again. It comes to this: you need milk instead of solid food. Anyone who lives on milk is still an infant, with no experience of what is right. Solid food is for adults, whose perceptions have been trained by long use to discriminate between good and evil. Let us stop discussing the rudiments of Christianity. We ought not to be laying the foundation all over again ... Instead, let us advance towards maturity.'[16]

The issue then, as now, appears to have been a general lack of faith-literacy, which is a challenge to spiritual life and mission and a serious hindrance to Christians in telling the gospel story and making connections between faith and life. The consequence is an inadequate engagement with contemporary thinking, culture and society in a world of secularism and apparently competing faiths.

In one of the parishes of which I was vicar, we planted a church in part of the parish that was neglected, both by the social services and the church. Through that church we began a regular home Bible study, led by my wife. She came home each week enthused by the down-to-earth engagement with the Scriptures demonstrated in that group. Tony Adamson describes a not untypical snatch of conversation in a similar context:

Leader: Why did Zacchaeus climb the tree?
First Member: To see better, I suppose. You've got to be careful, though. Our George climbed a tree in the park, fell out and broke his arm.
Second Member: Poor George, and he's such a nice lad, as well.
The Leader had intended a discussion on how unpopular people long to be accepted, but the resulting discussion centres on the problem of how a loving God can allow unjust suffering! Never mind, we'll get back to Zacchaeus later, after a cup of tea.[17]

It's not a matter of filling Christians with biblical and religious knowledge but of forming disciples for their vocation in the world. In many if not most of our churches people lack a sense of proportion about the things of God, and this is easily seen in the way relatively minor issues become major tests of faith because many lack a basic map, an overview. All that many of them get is disconnected bits and pieces from Sunday sermons, sometimes good, sometimes pretty useless; they are confused and disorientated, and they are not listening for the voice of God.

I hope you don't think I'm describing disciples who have lost their first love for God. Faith is first and foremost about a relationship with God and others, and relationships are first and foremost a matter of the heart. John Chrysostom (347-407) said,

'The Holy Scriptures were not given to us that we should enclose them in books, but that we should engrave them upon our hearts.'

Every disciple knows – often from personal experience of being loved into the kingdom of God – that the impact of a loving Christian community cannot be over-estimated. Every page of the New Testament speaks of the power of love – God's love for us, our love for God and one another. The apostolic witness is clearly of a world transformed by the power of God's love and love is at the very heart of the Gospel.

'My dear friends, let us love one another, because the source of love is God. Everyone who loves is a child of God and knows God, but the unloving know nothing of God, for God is love. This is how he showed his love among us: he sent his only Son into the world that we might have life through him. This is what love really is: not that we have loved God, but that he loved us and sent his Son as a sacrifice to atone for our sins. If God thus loved us, my dear friends, we also must love one another. God has never been seen by anyone, but if we love one another, he himself dwells in us; his love is brought to perfection within us.[18]

That, I propose, is one reason why God gave us necks, to connect the head with the heart and the heart with the head.

At the opposite extreme, education for its own sake is a trap into which it's possible to fall. J. John wrote of the Church of England's occasional potential to

'create graduates who can tell you about how the rhetorical and socio-historical setting of Galatians relates to the New View of St Paul but who have no idea how to console a dying person.'[19]

It's a tragic reality when teachers and preachers of the faith become gurus, and equally sad that their admirers become addicted to learning for its own sake. Disciples whose over-riding aim as Christians is simply to know more about the Bible are as useful as chocolate teapots!

So we find ourselves in the middle ground when it comes to understanding the faith we profess. St Paul wrestles with this dilemma in the two chapters of his First Letter to the Corinthians that surround his famous hymn in praise of love.[20] 'Yes, of course,' he writes, 'allow the Holy Spirit to work in you and do not prevent that work, but use your mind, too. Indeed you must use all the intellect God has given you, and don't neglect the activity of the Spirit.' Perhaps it is a result of the anti-intellectualism encouraged by the information revolution but knowing one's way around the Bible and being able to make sense of Christian doctrine and ethics is currently in short-supply.

Have you ever tried to do a double-sided jigsaw without the pictures? Even if you're very good at jigsaws, you might be tempted to give up after you've done a bit round the edge. And if your friends should pour scorn on your limited success, you'd have every right to remind them how difficult it is to get the pieces the right way up, let alone to get them to fit together without the pictures to work from! You'd probably say (and so would I) that it's quite an achievement to put together 50 pieces round the edge.

That's the kind of confusion in Christian thinking that we're facing in the churches of the 'West' or 'Global North', where a couple of generations or more of churchgoers have received very little help to put together the jigsaw of biblical theology; many feel content having simply put together a few pieces round the edges of belief before giving up. It's not really their fault: they don't have the big picture; they lacked proper training in the faith in the first place and consistent teaching after that to help them piece together what God has revealed of himself and his world. This failure to put together the jigsaw of primary Christian truth leads to theological disorientation. Many of the arch-heretics in the history of the Church have been people with a partial, distorted picture of God. Indeed, many ordinary Christians who turn up for church Sunday by Sunday find that after years of confusion they begin to get muddled about even the most vital aspects of our faith-relationship with God in Christ.[21]

As a preacher I know that one of the causes of boredom with sermons is feeble content; when sermons are trivial or irrelevant or lacking in the scope of eternity; when they are merely advice on how to cure the symptoms of the human predicament, how to deal with a sin here and a sin there – helpful hints for harmful habits – they are tiresome to hear. Gerhard Ebeling wrote,

'What an expenditure of effort is put into the preaching of the Christian faith up and down the land! But - again with exceptions - is it not the institutionally assured platitudes which are preached?'[22]

The prevailing culture in many churches is that education is for the kids, so adults don't need it any more. Too few disciples expose themselves to the Bible other than when they are in church and sermons are an inadequate way of meeting that need.

David Wood commented,

'The Church, and the whole Church rather than just the clergy as representative, is servant of the world. This means, ironically, that in this 'secular' age ordinary Christians will need to know more theology than ever before. The whole body of Christ needs to be theologically literate and intelligent, engaging in theological reflection on their everyday experiences, learning to think about their occupation in a Christian way and learning to choose in a Christian way. Ordinary men and women "who have to keep the faith and to survive in the grey world of business negotiations, trade union loyalties, party caucuses, popular journalism, competitive television" will be learning to think and choose in a Christian way, interpreting the hand of God, actively reaching out to take God's hand.'[23]

If you were to ask me what the most pressing need is, I'd say it's an overview of the Bible as a theatrical play. There's a huge cast, walk-on parts, minor characters, the supporting characters and the star; there are cleaners, scene-changers, props, lighting and front-of-house staff; all are needed if the play is to convey meaning and make an impression. So it is with the whole 'cast' of the Bible: the star is Jesus, the living Word of God; the supporting characters are people like Abraham, Moses, David, Isaiah, Mary, Peter, John, Paul; other parts might be taken by Job, John the Baptist, Mary Magdalene, Timothy ... Then there's the set, the lighting and the theatre (which may, in biblical terms, be Temple worship, the Graeco-Roman world, the Pharisees - you fill in the gaps) and, not least the audience. All make up the experience of the play, and our context will condition the impact of each scene but all are needed for an effective performance.

In a laudable desire to raise standards the churches of the 20th and 21st centuries we have focussed our attention on the need for quality training of future lay and ordained ministers rather than improving the biblical and theological literacy of all disciples. In fact, one of the difficulties faced by those training people for public ministry is the generally poor level of basic understanding of the faith by those who have been called and selected for training. This need to pay attention to all disciples was pointed out by a Church of England working group in 2015:

'There is a need for a radical and critical examination of the purpose of education and training for discipleship and lay ministry which takes these seriously in their own right rather than as a variant of ordained ministry; and also elucidates the difference between lay ministerial education and whole-life discipleship development.'

The danger in reading a book like this is that you might get the impression that discipleship is just for adults. I am an unapologetic baptizer of children and therefore I believe that discipleship can begin at the earliest of ages. Three great changes have occurred in considering the nurture of growing disciples. One is that children are more technologically articulare. The second is that they can no longer be 'seen but not heard' and are far more aware of their place in the church's family. The third is that it is now generally recognised that baptism is the full liturgical entry into the Church and to Holy Communion (whatever other important ceremonies such as confirmation or admission to membership there may be). This liberates churches to welcome children to the family meal – the Eucharist – at an early stage of faith, and leave in-depth teaching to the later teens.

Systematic teaching, however and whenever it is delivered, is known as 'catechesis' – a word that has enjoyed a recent resurrection. Good catechesis helps us to colour-in the picture of God. It is an educational process, a very ancient practice of extempore teaching by question-and-answer with its roots in the classical world of Socrates (470-399 BC), whose followers developed it into a kind of intellectual game, and Plato (428-347 BC), whose contribution was to develop the technique into a drama of ideas. It is found in the Wisdom literature of the Old Testament, particularly in the book of Job.

Catechesis is based on dialogue, possibly the most important form of teaching in the history of education. It is vital to story-telling because it lends reality to what may otherwise be abstract concepts. It's a building block of 'Godly play' and 'Open the Book' which give children the capacity to use religious language and discover meaning, and is also proving helpful in caring for people with dementia. In its straightforward question-and-answer form the dialogue is a basic element in New Testament teaching. The old story goes,

'Rabbi, why do you always answer a question with a question?'
'Why shouldn't I answer a question with a question?'

Jesus and his rabbinic contemporaries were familiar with the technique and it occurs frequently in the Gospels:

- Tell me, who do people say I am?
- Who do you say I am?
- Did the baptism of John come from heaven, or was it of human origin?
- Whose face and name are these?[24]

The New Testament letters contain strong echoes of the Stoic diatribes, in which imaginary objectors are answered by a teacher. In his correspondence St Paul, apostle to the Greek-speaking world, appears to conduct a conversation with himself on several occasions, notably in his Letter to the Romans. Reading these passages in dialogue form helps us to understand the argument:

Q: What advantage has the Jew? What is the value of circumcision?

A: Great, in every way. In the first place, the Jews were entrusted with the oracles of God.

Q: What if some of them were unfaithful? Will their faithlessness cancel the faithfulness of God?

A: Certainly not! God must be true though all men be proved liars ...

Q: If our injustice serves to confirm God's justice, what are we to say? Is it unjust of God (I speak of him in human terms) to bring retribution upon us?

A: Certainly not! If God were unjust, how could he judge the world?

Q: Again, if the truth of God is displayed to his greater glory through my falsehood, why should I any longer be condemned as a sinner? Why not indeed 'do evil that good may come', as some slanderously report me as saying?

A: To condemn such men as these is surely just.

Q: Well then, are we Jews any better off?

A: No, not at all! For we have already drawn up the indictment that all, Jews and Greeks alike, are under the power of sin. ...

Q: What room then is left for human pride?

A: It is excluded.

Q: And on what principle?

A: The keeping of the law would not exclude it, but faith does. ...

Q: Do you suppose God is the God of the Jews alone? Is he not the God of Gentiles also?

A: Certainly, of Gentiles also. For if the Lord is indeed one, he will justify the circumcised by their faith and the uncircumcised through their faith.

Q: Does this mean that we are using faith to undermine the law?

A: By no means: we are upholding the law.[25]

Paul was not alone: there has been a powerful Christian tradition of dialogue-teaching ever since, including such illustrious exponents as Augustine, Gregory, Anselm, Thomas Aquinas and John Wyclif, although it was Martin Luther who, between 1517 and 1525, invented what we know today as the catechism, a formal doctrinal play with two actors. This was an imaginative convergence of the two existing methods - extempore teaching by question-and-answer and formal dialogues - following generally the content that had developed in the later mediaeval children's primers. Richard Baxter (1615-91) who, like innumerable others also wrote a catechism, advised clergy that,

> 'The most godly people, therefore, in your congregations will find it worth their labour to learn the very words of a catechism.'[26]

This is no new-fangled method of communication in the Church!

Catechesis traditionally picked up the evangelism-baptism-education principles of the great commission,[27] and dealt with prayer (using the Lord's Prayer as the starting point), belief (starting with the Apostles' Creed) and behaviour (expounding the Ten Commandments and the Summary of the Law). Innumerable catechisms in the form in which we know them have been published since the sixteenth century.

Until the nineteenth century in many churches, particularly Anglican and Lutheran, Sunday afternoons were given over in part to catechising. At its best that did not mean parrot-fashion theology for children but using the catechism to provide a helpful introduction to more informal teaching. Educational theorists have been divided over the value of catechisms, so for decades they fell into disuse. Some, however, have come to the conclusion that becoming familiar with the language of faith – even memorising some of it – provides a disciple with the vocabulary with which to clarify the meaning of faith and a standard by which to judge the process of one's transformation. There may well be a lot of life left in the dialogue![2] An attempt at a catechism is found in chapter 10.

World awareness

Jesus could not have made it clearer that he expects his disciples to be transnational citizens.

'Go to every part of the world, and proclaim the gospel to the whole creation.'[29]

'You will receive power when the Holy Spirit comes upon you; and you will bear witness for me in Jerusalem, and throughout all Judaea and Samaria, and even in the farthest corners of the earth.'[30]

If it weren't so sad, a resolution of the General Assembly of the Church of Scotland in 1796 would be hilarious:

'... to spread abroad among barbarians and heathen natives the knowledge of the gospel seems to be highly preposterous, in so far as it anticipates, nay even reverses, the order of Nature.'

Seeing the world with Christian eyes, and seeing the Church with the eyes of the world adds depth to discipleship. I recall my first encounter with the developing world in one of the desperately poor parts of an otherwise affluent city, a place where some drove around in air-conditioned limousines while thousands of others lived and scavenged for food and re-cyclables on a stinking, smouldering rubbish-tip. I had seen other parts of the 'third world', but joining in a game of basketball with kids living in a level of poverty that I had not up to that point even begun to imagine (despite having seen it on television) changed my life for ever. I returned vowing that my children would witness this world before they could frame the foolish, partial view of the world that I had lived with before.

There is no space in the Church for racism because racism is a denial of the equal and infinite value that Christian disciples are called to place on every human being. In that sense, the issue is not about race but about recognising the supreme glory of God's creation: each and every human being made in his image. Racism occurs when people set a scale of values on others because they belong to different race, and put the highest value on their own. It's not only race, of course, that can be abused in this way, but arrogance about wealth, education, nation and ancestry can be equally destructive of the unity of the human family as children of God.

There are few parts of the world – there must be some but I don't know of any – unreached by the Christian gospel. Certainly there are plenty of people who have not experienced the gospel. Right from the beginning, the Church has been driven by a world-mission gene, and the New Testament story itself takes us from the capital of the Hebrew world, Jerusalem, to the capital of the Empire, Rome. In that story sometimes disciples were reluctant to step out beyond their comfort zone and found themselves forced by persecution to move. We see that happen in the Acts of the Apostles immediately following the execution of Stephen:

> 'That day was the beginning of a time of violent persecution for the church in Jerusalem; and all except the apostles were scattered over the country districts of Judaea and Samaria.'[31]

So, just one chapter later, Luke tells us that Christians had established themselves at Damascus in Samaria by the time Saul of Tarsus (Paul) was sent to exterminate them.[32] It was Paul whose commitment to a world-shaped mission and a gospel for all nations, working from his base at Antioch (contemporary Antakya), enabled non-Jews to become disciples by faith and baptism and led in time to the gospel being brought to our own shores by one route or another.

Having positive contacts with disciples in other parts of the world, particularly those that are different from us, has proved to be invaluable to the life of our churches. St Paul in his letters makes reference to support given by the gentile churches of the Mediterranean to the impoverished church in Judea, hit by famine during the reign of the Emperor Claudius (AD 41-54).[33] This support for one another as brothers and sisters in Christ has been one of the marks of the Church ever since – indeed, it was a mark of the pre-Christian Hebrew church, too. In a world of major inequality, there is a danger that the churches of the 'global north', despite recession, still see themselves as lady bountiful, and churches in poorer places still too readily accept this patronising attitude. In fact, it is the churches that are fighting for their lives that can give most from the bounty of their faith, hope and love.

Jon Kuhrt wrote of the danger to 'western' disciples of a detachment from reality that cannot be achieved, I believe, without a world perspective.

'Today there is widespread danger of our Christianity becoming detached from the daily realities of life. This is true right across the church spectrum, from modern charismatic movements to traditional churches. Religious form, such as the style of music, teaching, liturgy (as well as theological discussion) can easily become dominant over the ultimate function, which is to witness to the kingdom of God.

'As a result, a growing cycle of detachment develops between church culture and an increasingly outside world. This can lead to brittle beliefs, often fed by teaching and a culture that promotes an unbiblical divide between the sacred and the secular. Christians can find themselves with few resources to speak relevantly or confidently outside church environments and their faith can be easily shattered by the rough and tumble of the real world.

'Ultimately, a detached spirituality becomes deeply unsatisfying because instead of aiming to reach out and connect, as God has done to us, it simply fosters a religious sub-culture. It also provokes anxiety: as we lose the ability to connect our deepest beliefs relevantly to the world around us, we quickly lose confidence in the message itself.

'Community involvement directly challenges these cycles of detachment. When we seek to apply our beliefs by acting in situations to confront isolation, suffering and injustice, a different faith emerges.'34

Christian disciples in the next couple of generations will need to worry less about ecclesiastical niceties and concentrate on 'witness to the kingdom of God'. What do I suppose that witness will entail? High on the agenda will be world population growth which will be reduced only when decent healthcare, enough income, food, water and sanitation can be assured so that people can flourish with smaller families. Equally, pollution and climate change will be up there as top kingdom issues, despite a suicidal refusal of many today to confront these issues. Then there's extremism, conflict and migration of displaced people, about which we are just beginning to see the effects in Europe but which have been part of humanity's story in other parts of the world for a very long time. And education for all. Kuhrt is right that when disciples fail to connect their faith to the world and the critical issues facing it, they lose confidence in the gospel.

Youthfulness

The days when it was the exception for children brought up in Christian families to opt-out of discipleship have long gone. It's assumed in the Old Testament that parents would lead their children and teach them the faith, and this was normal for much of the Christian era where the church was established in any community. The Hebrews' image of themselves as a vine was all about growth and new shoots:

'Israel is like a spreading vine with ripening fruit. ... I shall be as dew to Israel that they may flower like the lily, strike root like the poplar, and put out fresh shoots, that they may be as fair as the olive and fragrant as Lebanon. Israel will again dwell in my shadow; they will grow vigorously like grain, they will flourish like a vine, and be as famous as the wine of Lebanon.'[35]

Today we live in an age of choices and one in which young people are fed from an early age with three views of religion: first, science has disproved it; second, all faiths and spiritualities are expressions of the same thing; third, faith is an interesting cultural phenomenon and churches are reserves for those who can't throw the habit. A fourth might be a question: 'Why would you go to a church on Sunday when there's so much more to do – shopping, for a start?' Religious education is OK because it teaches people to think in an abstract way, but keep faith out of it!

This is where the rubber really hits the road. No one is going to persuade those teachers and others who are convinced that it is their duty to slag off faith that they should stop. The distinctiveness of Christianity, in particular that it is about what God has done for you, not what you can do for God, is difficult to convey at first, and knowledge even of the basic texts and practices of Christianity is limited. The more the world changes, particularly with accessible technology, the more parts of the inherited Church looks weird; yet rightly the Church doesn't want to abandon its great heritage of liturgy, literature, poetry, music and the visual arts.

It's an uphill struggle but here's where discipleship comes in. Forget the teachers and preachers: tell me, is it true? If you say Jesus is Lord, tell me about what that means as a disciple. If you assert that God is love, show me what that means by the way you behave as a disciple. Don't explain to me about carrying your cross, carry it! In other words, be a disciple.

If I seem to have painted a negative picture, numerically at the moment (with some highly significant exceptions) it is a faithful portrait. But there are signs in many places of new life. Take an example like 'Friday Serv', an all-age, all-inclusive act of worship in which people come together on Friday evening to pray, to learn, to eat and to welcome outsiders, particularly those who would find the regular church services difficult and alienating. And 'Soul Food', a gathering on Sunday evenings in an ancient church to eat together, share some interactive God-focussed activity, and pray; run by an ecumenical group, this draws in those in need and the many who would usually find the church door intimidating. If the Church is ever to connect the heart of what it does - love God and love people - with younger generations it must welcome new initiatives, 'fresh expressions of being church'.

Young adults tend to possess two particular and valuable attributes: they are altruistic and they can sniff out a phoney at 100 metres. Altruism is a friend to prayer and action for the coming of the kingdom of God. But what about hypocrisy? A church that says all the right things about God and the world might attract young people at first, particularly if the music is reasonable and the environment is congenial, but it will lose them if they come across disciples who don't live up to their profession. When I come across churches with numbers of younger people, I look for the reasons. Yes, they may have understood the need to soften the impact of church a little – we all need to do that – but at heart what those churches are good at is kingdom discipleship with integrity.

Ecumenical collaboration

The disciples of Jesus have made something of a habit of splitting into groups. Some people blame the 16th century Reformation but it had been going on long before that. Clearly from his letters to the early Christian communities, St Paul had to face divisions in these local churches to which he was writing – the Corinthians in particular seem to have been a headstrong bunch! Repeatedly the New Testament urges Christians to recognise one another, despite personal preferences and differences, for two reasons. First because they are the 'body of Christ', an image to which Paul resorts in different ways in three of his letters,[36] so there should be no alternative but to recognise other parts of Christ's body. And second, because unity supports mission: when disciples disagree and refuse fellowship (communion) with one another, observers ask, 'What's the use of the gospel if it doesn't improve relationships?' and, 'How am I supposed to choose between the different versions of Christianity on offer?'

In his Letter to the Ephesians, St Paul gets at these important principles when he writes of

'living up to our calling. Be humble always and gentle, and patient too, putting up with one another's failings in the spirit of love. Spare no effort to make fast with bonds of peace the unity which the Spirit gives. There is one body and one Spirit, just as there is one hope held out in God's call to you; one Lord, one faith, one baptism; one God and Father of all, who is over all and through all and in all.

'... until we all attain to the unity inherent in our faith and in our knowledge of the Son of God.'

And he writes of maintaining

> 'the truth in a spirit of love; so shall we fully grow up into Christ. He is the head, and on him the whole body depends. Bonded and held together by every constituent joint, the whole frame grows through the proper functioning of each part, and builds itself up in love.'[37]

Disciples generally disagree less these days about doctrine: perhaps that's because doctrine is not generally well understood – see above. These days we disagree more about emphasis and style. Seasoned churchmanship-spotters will know by now what label to attach to me; it's not difficult for those who study the signs. But it is singularly unhelpful for me to attach a label to myself. If I were to say I favoured a 'catholic' approach, I would have grabbed that word for myself and assert that my opinions represent a holistic view of the church, implying that others aren't properly connected in the way I see it. If I were to say I favoured an 'evangelical' approach, I would have grabbed that word for myself and assert that my opinions give priority to the gospel in the church, implying that others don't give the gospel priority in the way I see it. Self-adhesive labels are never helpful.

Many disciples of Jesus today are happy to move across denominations, and that is not unhealthy. I was vicar for some time of a church that sometimes felt like a transit-camp because people of many traditions and denominations would arrive, often spiritually exhausted, looking for something special that they needed at that time, and later they would move on, sometimes back to where they had come from, sometimes elsewhere. Without seeming to condone ecclesiastical tourism – 'If it's Wednesday, this must be the C of E' – a more accepting approach to the old divisions is vital in a secular age. One of the reasons I find my self so much at home in Anglicanism, having discovered it at much the same time as I found faith during my teens, is that at best it is so accepting, that the threshold of entry is low, and therefore the threshold of exit is equally low.

Numbers

In the film Toy Story, Buzz Lightyear, in a crisis, says, 'This is no time to panic.' Woody replies, 'This is a great time to panic!' I'm tempted to think Woody might be right. The average British churchgoer is at or older than the age at which most people retire from work, and that's a numerical time-bomb. Numbers do matter, even though they are not the primary goal of growth because if the church declines seriously so will its impact for good in society. Growth is in God's hands, as St Paul commented of a colleague with whom he seems to have had a difficult relationship,

'I planted the seed, and Apollos watered it; but God made it grow. ... We are fellow-workers in God's service; and you are God's garden.'[38]

The two post World War II decades into which half of British churchgoers were born was the high water mark of church attendance in the western world but, as has been noted, that period of popular traditional churchgoing began to decline during the 1960's. There remain some in our churches today who cling to the belief that if only we returned to what we were doing in Coronation year, 1953, all would be well. That thinking is off with the fairies!

The *Talking Jesus* research in England in 2015 and 2016 pointed to 43% of the adult population (59% of young people) identifying as non-Christian, 51% (28% young people) as non-practising Christian, and 7% (13% young people) as practising Christian. Practising Christians are roughly equally divided between the under 55's and those who are older. 33% of non-Christian adults (45% young people) say they don't know a practising Christian. Interestingly, perhaps reflecting the growth of Islam and the teaching of comparative religion in schools, 29% of adults and young people describe Jesus as a prophet, though 22% of adults (27% of young people) think he's either a mythical or fictional character.[39]

Christian leaders are bombarded by statistics about this growing parish or that declining church, each offering the key to understanding growth and decline, and people like me are sceptical. So much time and energy is spent on the fundamentally internal exercise of trying to make the church grow. Patterns of church attendance have been and are changing; nevertheless, without numbers the institution cannot be sustained and a very new shape will need to appear.

It is always dangerous to set numerical targets. Eugene H Peterson has wisely commented,

> 'In a capitalist/consumerist economy, we unthinkingly evaluate progress in terms of larger numbers. As we become habituated in this mind-set, we pay attention only to those parts of reality that we can measure with numbers. We get used to using the word growth in this context.
> 'But we forget that growth is a biological, not an arithmetical, metaphor. Growth in biology has to do with timing, passivity, waiting, proportion, maturity. There is a proper size to each thing. There are proportions to be attended to. It is an exceedingly complex and mysterious thing, this process of growth. ...

'Reticence, then – a healthy respect for limits – is a requisite pastoral skill. An enthusiasm for God's unlimited grace requires as its corollary a developed sensitivity to human limits. We have to know when and where to stop.'[40]

So, what might happen in the future? Some of us have been asking this question since the last century. One possibility is that the Church in these lands will decline over many years until we reach a point of extinction. A simplistic reading of the statistics might point to this and many of us would probably be dead before it took place. However, it's not likely to happen that way because institutions like churches do not fade away gradually. They drop to critical mass, to the point where the life of the body is not sustainable, and then they collapse under their own weight. Congregations become too small to pay for shared ministry and to maintain buildings, so the weakest go to the wall. A few people move to another church in order to be part of a Christian community, but some don't bother. A few strong churches survive because they have the vision, money, viable congregations, a population base and some transfer-growth. Believe me, if all this happens, some people will say that no one warned them!

In this context – and I am far from denying the seriousness of the situation as some of the Church's weaker branches face possible closure and finances generally are precarious – there are dangers that we will focus on the wrong kind of self-referential programme of internal renewal. Here I find myself in the realm of paradox because I want to see renewal and growth, both in depth and maturity, but I am fearful of strategies that pander to an internal market. I am also fearful that people who may otherwise be receptive to the gospel of new life in Christ may well be put off by a tone of desperation in the voices of some Christian disciples.

Where might we look for some biblical insights? In the late 7th and early 6th centuries BC Jeremiah was called by God to proclaim an impossible message, the conquest of Judah by the Babylonians, and the destruction of the City of Jerusalem and its Temple, such that he became thoroughly depressed. The Temple was indeed closed down, the holy city deprived of its status, numbers of the people deported, and the exile lasted two or three generations. However, the prospect of institutional exile was not simply a message of disaster and despair. The letter sent by Jeremiah to the exiles in Babylon encouraged them to flourish in the place of their exile:

'These are the words of the Lord of Hosts the God of Israel: To all the exiles whom I deported from Jerusalem to Babylon: Build houses and live in them; plant gardens and eat the produce; ... Increase there and do not dwindle away. Seek the welfare of any city to which I have exiled you, and pray to the Lord for it; on its welfare your welfare will depend.'[41]

And his purchase of land[42] was a demonstration of hope and restoration that would take place after exile. In due time, after a period of correction, the people would indeed seek the Lord, find him and be restored to the land.

'I shall bring you back safe from afar ... For I am with you to save you, says the Lord. ... I shall discipline you only as you deserve, I shall not leave you wholly unpunished.'[43]

Today's disciples need to be awake to the possibility that something similar might be in store for us in the 'global north': the divine closure of the institutional church or - and this is certainly worse - the closure of all that isn't financially viable! The whole of my Christian life and public ministry has been based on the conviction that God has a great future for his Church, even for the institution, and it still is; but I have to ask myself whether there are signs that God may have different plans. If our aspirations for growth are all about saving the Church, instead of giving ourselves to God and offering good news to the world, we will simply find ourselves drawn into a struggle for survival. In all sincerity we may be looking for the renewal of the system instead of searching for the coming of the kingdom of God. In doing so, the danger is that we may fail to notice the King at work. That danger should not be dismissed.

At the same time we can see that there are exciting new expressions of Church life springing up everywhere, real beacons of growth and hope when they recognise themselves and are recognised as fully part of the Church. We know of cell groups, inspirational worship, church plants, Messy Churches, Alpha and Pilgrim courses, loving pastoral care, committed praying, relevant teaching and good nurturing. These are important indicators that the Church is less concerned about itself and the preservation of the institution, real signs of renewal and growth. Contemporary disciples will be there.

The fresh wind of the Holy Spirit is blowing in many places. So we do not hold up our hands in despair but keep our eyes open for where new life and blessing is appearing, discern the ways in which the inherited treasures of the past can enrich the future, give them every possible encouragement and support, and allow some things to die.

'Growth,' wrote Cardinal Newman, 'is the only evidence of life.'[44]

Almighty God,
who sent your Holy Spirit
to be the life and light of your Church:
open our hearts to the riches of your grace,
that we may bring forth the fruit of the Spirit
and live the good news we proclaim;
through Jesus Christ your Son our Lord.
Amen.

(Collect of the 9th Sunday after Trinity, altd.)

References

1. 1 Samuel 2. 20; Luke 2. 40.
2. Psalm 103. 15, 16.
3. Matthew 13. 1-43; see also Mark 4 and Luke 8, etc.
4. For instance 1 Corinthians 14. 20; 1 Peter 2. 2.
5. For instance Colossians 2. 19; 2 Thessalonians 1. 3.
6. John 15. 8-10, 16, 17.
7. John 15. 5; Acts 2. 42.
8. Monty Pithon's Flying Circus.
9. From the Church Times, 20 August, 1992, 'Truth for our Time'.
10. 2 Peter 3. 18.
11. Ephesians 4. 13, 15; Colossians 1. 28.
12. 1 Corinthians 13. 13.
13. 1593-1633
14. A recurring metaphor, particularly in Augustine's Exposition of the Psalms.
15. Colossians 2. 12-15.
16. Hebrews 5.12 – 6.2.
17. Inner City Evangelism, Grove Evangelism No. 22, 1993; and see Luke 19. 1-10.
18. 1 John 4. 7-12.
19. J. John: The Good Old Church of England, 2015.
20. 1 Corinthians 12 - 14.
21. See Robert Paterson: Short, Sharp and Off the Point, MARC Europe 1987.
22. The Nature of Faith, Collins, 1961, p 15.
23. David Wood: Poet, Priest and Prophet, CTBI, 2002, quoting Bishop John V. Taylor.
24. Mark 8. 27, 29; 11. 30; 12. 16
25. Romans 3. 1-9; 27-31.
26. Richard Baxter: The Reformed Pastor, (1655).

27. Matthew 28. 19,20.
28. See Robert Paterson: Short, Sharp and Off the Point, MARC Europe 1987.
29. Mark 16: 15; see also Matthew 28. 19.
30. Acts 1. 8.
31. Acts 8. 1.
32. Acts 9.
33. See Acts 11. 27-30; Galatians 2. 10; 1 Corinthians 16. 1-4; 2 Corinthians 8 - 9.
34. Integrated Faith, The Shaftesbury Society, 2004.
35. Hosea 10. 1; 14. 5-7.
36. Romans 12; 1 Corinthians 12; Ephesians 4.
37. Ephesians 4. 1-6, 13, 15, 16.
38. 1 Corinthians 3. 6, 9.
39. See talkingjesus.org
40. Under the Unpredictable Plant, 1992, Eerdmans, pp 138-9.
41. Jeremiah 29. 4-7.
42. Jeremiah 32.
43. Jeremiah 30. 10, 11.
44. Quoting Thomas Scott 'The Force of Truth'.

9 Called to Live

What is the purpose of being a disciple of Jesus? We ought to be better people as a result – and that can't be bad - but what's it all for? Is there a job description and an ultimate goal?

The Gospels repeatedly use the expression 'the kingdom of God' or 'the kingdom of heaven'. The two expressions seem to mean more-or-less the same thing, with Matthew generally favouring 'kingdom of heaven'. It's a tricky idea: some people think the kingdom means heaven, and there are suggestions of that in the Gospels, so they focus their prayers on making sure they and others get there. Others tend to see the kingdom in terms of righteousness, and that's equally justifiable, so they focus their prayers on social and international justice. It's very difficult to get the idea out of our minds that the kingdom is a place, though theologically we should define 'kingdom' as 'reign' or 'régime', which may go some way to help us conceive of it in less spatial terms. Let's look at the prophet Ezekiel's final oracle as a preview of the kingdom that Jesus told us to pray for.

'The man brought me back to the entrance of the temple, and I saw a spring of water issuing towards the east from under the threshold of the temple; for the temple faced east. The water was running down along the south side, to the right of the altar. He took me out through the north gate and led me round by an outside path to the east gate of the court, and I saw water was trickling from the south side. With a line in his hand the man went out eastwards, and he measured off a thousand cubits and made me walk through the water; it came up to my ankles. Again he measured a thousand cubits and made me walk through the water; it came up to my knees. He measured another thousand and made me walk through the water; it was up to my waist. He measured another thousand, and it was a torrent I could not cross; the water had risen and was deep enough to swim in, a torrent impossible to cross. "Take note of this, O man," he said, and led me back to the bank. When I got to the bank I saw a great number of trees on each side. He said to me, "This water flows out to the region lying east, and down to the Arabah; it will run into the sea whose waters are noxious, and they will be made fresh. ... Beside the torrent on either bank fruitful trees of every kind will grow. Their leaves will not wither, nor will their fruit fail; they will bear fruit early every month, for the water for them flows from the sanctuary; their fruit is for food and their leaves for healing." "[1]

As Jeremiah had said, around 573 BC Jerusalem and its Temple was devastated, the people scattered, leaderless and in poverty; it was a new wilderness, no less barren than the wilderness that Moses, Aaron and their people wandered through when the people fled from slavery. A new prophet, Ezekiel, living among the exiles in Babylon, is shown a a vision of a new temple, and sees the glory of the Lord enter it. From beneath the temple water gushes out, becomes a stream, a river like the one that flowed through Eden in the stories of creation; soon it is too deep to wade in and the prophet has to swim; it pours out from the temple and the city into the desert; refreshes the wilderness and even de-salinates the Dead Sea. It is a picture of the promise to Abraham[2] - St Paul's 'gospel to Abraham'[3] – that all the nations would be refreshed by the flow of blessing from God's people.

Ezekiel's oracle is full of the symbolism of the end times, comparable with the final chapters of the New Testament. This is John's vision in the Revelation with its word-pictures of a new creation and the city of God, a vision offered to the early church in another exile or wilderness of persecution. In this city of God described by John there is no temple: the presence of God and the Lamb is its glory; there is no further need of religion. Like Ezekiel's vision, and like the picture of the river in the Garden of Eden, there is a river here, too - and notice the similarities with Ezekiel:

'The angel showed me the river of the water of life, sparkling like crystal, flowing from the throne of God and of the Lamb, down the middle of the city's street. On either side of the river stood a tree of life ... whose leaves are for the healing of the nations.'[4]

The river of the water of life enables the land on the banks of the river to flourish and trees to grow, not like the tree in the Garden of Eden whose fruit brought moral responsibility and condemnation, but trees whose leaves bring healing to the nations. The picture of a river is different from that of a kingdom but both illustrate what lies behind the teaching of Jesus.

Jesus posed a question about life's true values:

'Can anxious thought add a single day to your life? ... Set your mind on God's kingdom and his justice before everything else, and all the rest will come to you as well.'[5]

Christian disciples not only pray every day in the Lord's Prayer for God's kingdom to come but are also called to search for it. What does it mean to look for the kingdom in terms of our daily lives and the people among whom we live? It means being 'expectant and watchful for the signs of God's presence',[6] being alert to where God is at work, where the healing Spirit is flowing in barren places, and diverting some of our energies into enabling God's river to irrigate dry lands.

The Church is so good at looking for the river of God in holy places and at religious events – it's become second nature – that we've stopped looking elsewhere. But when we pray for God's kingdom to come, we're praying first of all to see signs of the river wherever it is flowing; to pray for insight to see the Spirit at work in the hidden, secular places, the wildernesses and dead seas that we Christians often fear and leave to others because these are places where we feel out of control. The purpose of making a search for the kingdom our priority is that, when we see God at work, wherever that is, we can join in bringing his healing. So the river of God, the flowing of the Spirit, alerts us to God's kingdom among us.

I think of Jenny, a market-trader who was persuaded to join an 'Alpha' course. She had no previous Christian background but came to know and love the Lord Jesus Christ. She still gets moments of depression but now she knows, 'God is by my side. If I'm feeling down, I just speak to him.' Jenny knows in her deepest being that the kingdom has come to her and she longs for others to share it.

Between these two oracles in Ezekiel and Revelation, separated by more than 600 years, is John's account of an encounter between Jesus and a Samaritan woman living with her sixth man.

> 'Whoever drinks the water I shall give will never again be thirsty. The water that I shall give will be a spring of water within, welling up and bringing eternal life.'

And on a slightly later occasion, he declares,

> 'Let anyone who is thirsty come to me, and let the one who believes in me drink. ... Out of the believer's heart shall flow rivers of living water.'[7]

(John adds a note explaining that by 'living water' Jesus meant the Spirit.)

Jesus seems to be drawing on Ezekiel's vision of the river of life flowing from the Temple, the only place on earth where God was willing to say he dwelt. The Temple in Jerusalem was destroyed by the Roman powers in AD 70, but in John's Gospel (written after that event) Jesus speaks of the destruction of the Temple in terms of the destruction of his own body on the cross and of his resurrection as the rebuilding of the Temple three days later.[8]   Thus he identified himself as the place on earth where God dwells and in whom reconciliation takes place. Later in the same gospel[9] Jesus describes himself as 'the vine', an image used to describe the people among whom God made his home, a bold claim to be the embodiment of the people among whom God dwells. Thus it is that he speaks of the water of the Spirit welling up from within, bringing eternal life and forming rivers of living water.

God dwells among the people of Jesus. Add to that St Paul's description of the physical body of a believer as 'a temple of the Holy Spirit'.[10] You and I, as Christian disciples, people who have answered Christ's call to follow him, are therefore each a living temple of God and we 'dwell'[11] in Jesus the vine; we are wells of the living water of the Holy Spirit, who bubbles up within. We are never made disciples for our own sakes, never even for the sake of the Church, but to be the rivers of his Spirit flowing out to a thirsty world.

Being a disciple lies behind everything you are and do; it's why nurturing new faith or giving a helping hand to limping disciples and caring for weary disciples is so important for the Church. Someone nurtured you, someone was there to lean on when your spiritual leg was in plaster, someone came alongside you when you thought you'd had enough. If we look to the Church to heal people and nations, to build the kingdom for which we pray every day, to be the rivers of blessing we are called to be, then it is our calling to be on the lookout for and swim in the flood of the Spirit of God, as it flows through ourselves and others. The river of living water is a symbol of potential, of the possibility that, insofar as we are immersed in the Spirit of Christ, the Church can bring refreshing life to individuals and communities, can continue to bring about the kingdom of God, to be the well of Jesus' life-giving water, a flood of promised blessing to the nations. The job description of the disciple is to search and pray for the kingdom and so make Christ visible.

When Christians gather for worship one element of their coming together is usually penitence: words, perhaps music, even actions, expressing to God and one another that we are sinners in need of forgiveness. In many traditions that will be followed by a declaration of God's pardon set in the context of the reading of scripture. (Some Christians also make a habit of one-to-one confession before a priest.) What matters is that we put it out there: we are sinners, we wish we didn't sin so frequently, we ask the God of all mercy both to wipe the slate clean and to send his Spirit alongside to help us sin less often, and we recognise that ultimately we will be freed from sin. The First Letter of Peter puts it well:

'He [Jesus] carried our sins in his own person on the gibbet, so that we might cease to live for sin and begin to live for righteousness. By his wounds you have been healed.'[12]

Repentance is a stopping-off point on the road to holiness, a road from which we often take our own diversions but to which God calls us to return again and again. Holiness – or specialness, being 'question-mark people' – is all about becoming more like Christ, and therefore making Christ more visible.

When we gather to celebrate the Eucharist, the Lord's Supper, we are powerfully reminded of the Lord Jesus, his cross and resurrection, and come to be fed with his life. For centuries Christians scholars argued whether, how and to what extent Christ is present in the bread and wine; thank God those times are past. What matters in the celebration is summed up in another title we use for the service, 'Holy Communion'. That's a clue as to the purpose of celebrating the sacrament: it is to make us more holy by bringing us into close communion with the Lord or, in other words, to make Christ more present and visible in our lives today than he was yesterday. The bread and the cup are less sacred than those who receive them, and the purpose of the sacrament is not to consecrate some bread and wine but to consecrate God's treasures, people, for whom his Son has given his life. George Herbert described this true purpose of the sacrament in one of his more difficult poems:

Then of this also I am sure
That thou didst all those pains endure
To'abolish Sinn, not Wheat.[13]

St Paul puts the Christ-likeness of his people in the context of God's eternal purposes for the whole of creation, likening us to Jesus' brothers and sisters:

'For those whom God knew before ever they were, he also ordained to share the likeness of his Son, so that he might be the eldest among a large family of brothers; and those whom he foreordained, he also called, and those whom he called he also justified, and those whom he justified he also glorified.'[14]

That notion of Christ-likeness leading us, his brothers and sisters, to be glorified is a familiar theme of Paul's, not least in his letters to the Corinthians, and it is almost shocking in its audacity. Becoming more Christ-like does not simply affect our moral and spiritual judgements, the way we conduct our lives, but also grants us a share in the glory of the Lord.

'I speak God's hidden wisdom, his secret purpose framed from the very beginning to bring us to our destined glory.'[15]
'... we are being transformed into his likeness with ever-increasing glory, through the power of the Lord who is the Spirit.'[16]
'For the God who said, 'Out of darkness light shall shine,' has caused his light to shine in our hearts, the light which is knowledge of the glory of God in the face of Jesus Christ.'[17]

There's more. For the whole universe there is the promise that our Lord Jesus will come again in glory. The images of 'the Day of the Lord' in the Bible are many and varied.[18] That day is the arrival of the King and the revealing of the power and glory of the Lord when what is true in heaven will be fulfilled on earth. Here is a link with the Lord's Prayer, in which Jesus teaches us to pray for the kingdom to come and God's will to be done 'on earth as in heaven' or, literally, 'as in heaven also on earth'.

For the disciple of Jesus there is a personal promise and hope of fulfilment. The living water of the Spirit is given that we may be drawn to Christ and Christ may be drawn to us. The first disciples of Jesus must have been aware of the risk of abandoning ambition and security for the greater purpose that the writer of the Letter to the Hebrews memorably expresses two or three generations later.

'Here we have no lasting city, but we are seekers after the city which is to come.'[20]

It is as though he is comparing the people who refused the call of Christ and stayed where they were with the commitment of the first disciples in the three years of Jesus' earthly ministry. One group holding on to the security of what they knew because it seemed to guarantee their future; the other willing to be itinerant, knowing that ultimate security comes by letting go. The image is a parable of all discipleship, and points on towards the promise of eternal life.[19] The journey that began with the call leads beyond death to humanity's true home.

Jesus Christ was crucified along with two thieves. Their reactions to their predicament have become symbolic of the reaction of many to the Christian gospel:

'One of the criminals hanging there taunted him: "Are not you the Messiah? Save yourself, and us." But the other rebuked him: "Have you no fear of God? You are under the same sentence as he is. In our case it is plain justice; we are paying the price for our misdeeds. But this man has done nothing wrong." And he said, "Jesus, remember me when you come to your throne." Jesus answered, "Truly I tell you: today you will be with me in Paradise." '[21]

The impact of this passage is dulled by familiarity but it is staggering. Here are men in excruciating pain at the end of their lives recognising the Messiah. In the face of imminent death, one of them wants the King to save his skin, whereas the other asks the King to remember him in the eternal reign of God unbroken by death.

On the eve of that crucifixion, Jesus prayed, in words that were, perhaps, mingled with commentary,

'This is eternal life: to know you the only true God, and Jesus Christ whom you have sent.'[22]

It is an affirmation that is reminiscent of the First Letter of John,

'This is the witness: God has given us eternal life, and this life is found in his Son. He who possesses the Son possesses life; he who does not possess the Son of God does not possess life.'[23]

That's the ultimate call of the disciple and goal of the kingdom: eternal life that starts now and a promise of a world made whole, God's creation totally renewed and restored for all eternity. It is the gift of the glorious liberty of the children of God – 'the inextinguishable laughter of heaven'[24] and 'the fragile hope for something better on the other side of pain and death'.[25] It is being beyond place and time, the eternal fulfilment of being a disciple.

'High up in the North, in the land called Svithjod, there stands a rock. It is 100 miles high and 100 miles wide. Once every 1,000 years, a little bird comes to this rock to sharpen its beak. When the rock has thus been worn away, then a single day of eternity will have gone by.'[26]

For me, the pinnacle of the writings of the Apostle Paul is chapter 8 of his Letter to the Romans. Long ago, when I was a curate, the vicar, my boss, suggested that memorizing the whole chapter would add depth to my discipleship and ministry, and he was right. With one glorious idea rushing over into the next like a mountain stream, Paul writes of the privileges of being 'sons and daughters of God' (rather than 'children' to make the point that we are heirs, not young adults, and more than children of creation). He sees beyond the frustrations and shackles of mortal life, the groanings of our orphaned nature, towards the liberation of the adopted sons and daughters of God secured in the promise of the Spirit.

'I reckon that the sufferings we now endure bear no comparison with the glory, as yet unrevealed, which is in store for us. The created universe is waiting with eager expectation for God's sons and daughters to be revealed.

It was made subject to frustration, not of its own choice but by the will of him who subjected it, yet with the hope that the universe itself is to be freed from the shackles of mortality and is to enter upon the glorious liberty of the children of God. Up to the present, as we know, the whole created universe in all its parts groans as if in the pangs of childbirth. What is more, we also, to whom the Spirit is given as the first-fruits of the harvest to come, are groaning inwardly while we look forward eagerly to our adoption, our liberation from mortality. It was with this hope that we were saved. Now to see something is no longer to hope: why hope for what is already seen? But if we hope for something we do not yet see, then we look forward to it eagerly and with patience.'[27]

This is the goal of discipleship, the end of the journey that begins with Jesus' call: 'Follow me!'

That sense of call from start to fulfilment is well expressed in one of Ally Barrett's powerful hymns:[28]

> Gracious God, your love has found us,
> bound us, set us free.
> Take our lives, transform us into
> all that we can be.
> *Call us, one and all, together,*
> *now and evermore, we pray.*
>
> Call us to be Christ-revealing,
> radiant with your light;
> generous as a hilltop city,
> visible and bright.
> *Call us, one and all, together …*
>
> Call us all to live the kingdom,
> active here and now;
> Life affirming, world-renewing.
> Church above, below.
> *Call us, one and all, together …*

Call us all in love discerning,
strong in word and deed;
sent, commissioned, gladly serving
all who are in need.
Call us, one and all, together ...

Call us as your loved disciples:
learning, growing, fed;
Send us out, as new apostles,
Leading as we're led.
Call us, one and all, together ...

Call us deeply, touch our souls through
worship, prayer and word,
teach our minds to feel in echo
myst'ries yet unheard.
Call us, one and all, together ...

Call us, as you called creation
when the world began,
Guide our hearts' imagination
to your loving plan.
*Call us, one and all, together,
now and evermore, we pray.*

Almighty God,
you have made us for yourself,
and our hearts are restless
till they find their rest in you:
teach us to offer ourselves to your service,
that here we may have your peace,
and in the world to come
may see you face to face;
through Jesus Christ your Son our Lord.
Amen.

(Collect of the 17th Sunday after Trinity)

References

1. Ezekiel 47. 1-8, 12.
2. Genesis 12. 3.
3. Galatians 3. 6-9.
4. Revelation 22. 1, 2.
5. Matthew 6. 27, 33; Luke 12. 25, 31.
6. Common Worship: The Ordination of Deacons.
7. John 4. 14; 7. 37, 38.
8. John 2. 18-22.
9. John 15. 1-10.
10. 1 Corinthians 3. 17; 6. 19.
11. 'dwell' is difficult to translate – perhaps 'abide', 'remain fully part of', 'stay joined to'.
12. 1 Peter 2. 24.
13. The H. Communion.
14. Romans 8. 29, 30.
15. 1 Corinthians 2. 7.
16. 2 Corinthians 3. 18b.
17. 2 Corinthians 4. 6.
18. See Matthew chapters 7, 24, 26; Luke ch 10; John chs 7, 9, 12; Acts chs 1, 2; 1 Corinthians chs 1, 5, 15, 16; 2 Corinthians chs 1, 7; Philippians chs 1, 2; Ephesians ch 1; 1 Thessalonians chs 2, 3, 4, 5; 2 Thessalonians chs 1, 2; 1 Timothy ch 4; 2 Timothy chs 1, 4; Titus ch 2; Hebrews chs 1, 3, 9, 12; James ch 5; 1 Peter chs 1, 4; 2 Peter chs 1, 3; 1 John ch 2; Revelation ch 3.
19. Matthew 19. 16-30; Mark 10. 17-31; Luke 18. 18-30.
20. Hebrews 13. 14.
21. Luke 23. 39-43.
22. John 17. 3.
23. 1 John 5. 11, 12.
24. Sir Thomas Browne (1605-82).
25. Michael Gerson: The Last Temptation, 2018.
26. Hendrik Willem Van Loon: The Story of Mankind.
27. Romans 8. 18-25.
28. See https://reverendally.org/reverendallys-hymns Tune: Wulfstan Way or Guiting Power.

10 Called to Learn

A Short Catechism

This catechism is divided into four sections:
1. Being Disciples
2. The Creed
3. The Commandments
4. The Presence of God.

A traditional way to teach a catechism is to sub-divide each section and use a few questions-and-answers on each occasion to explore the biblical material on which the teaching is based. This will usually take place over an extended period of time. The dialogue itself merely sets the scene and is not as important as the topics raised. A few suggested biblical texts are provided but there are many others.

The catechism could be used not only in a teaching environment but also in the context of worship using two speakers.

O God,
who commanded light to shine out of darkness:
shine in our hearts,
to bring us to the light
of the knowledge of your glory
shining in the face
of Jesus Christ our Lord.
Amen.

(From St Paul in 2 Corinthians 4)

1 Being Disciples

Q We have come together to discover more about being a disciple of Jesus Christ. Let's start with creation.
What do we mean when we say God created the universe from nothing?

A We understand that God alone is the source of all that exists. God created everything good.[1]

Q We are human beings.
Tell me what we mean when we say we are created in God's image?

A Human beings have been created with the capacity to make free choices: to reason, to love, to form relationships and to create.

Q That's good. Is there any problem with that?

A Unfortunately, yes, there is. Our freedom means that we sin, by which I mean we naturally rebel against God, think and do what is wrong and fail to do what is right. [2]

Q How does being a disciple of Jesus help in this predicament?

A In Christ we find forgiveness, the power of the Spirit to live for others, and adoption as sons and daughters of God.

Q How is that relationship with God and his world re-established?

A By faith in Jesus Christ, my Lord and Lord of all.[3]

Q For those baptized as children, promises were made on their behalf.
Adults take on these promises for themselves.
You now wish to make these promises for yourself.
What are the promises?

A The promises are in two parts: first, to turn away from sin and reject evil.

Q What does it mean to turn away from sin and evil?

A We recognise in ourselves a natural tendency to wander away from God and what he wants us to be as his children;[4] sometimes we give in to temptations to evil thoughts, words and actions. It is important to seek forgiveness and peace with God and our neighbours.[5]

Q What do you mean by forgiveness?

A Forgiveness is cleaning away our sin and the guilty feelings that accompany it, giving us a fresh start. The New Testament clearly teaches that 'Christ Jesus came into the world to save sinners';[6] and that 'When anyone sins, we have an advocate to plead with the Father for us: Jesus Christ, the righteous one, by whom our sins are forgiven'.[7]

Q You said there were two parts to the promises in baptism: what else?

A The second part is to turn to Christ as Saviour and trust in him as Lord.

Q Another word for 'turn' is 'conversion'. What does that mean?

A His Son our Lord Jesus came to rescue us and turn us back to his way. He turns us away from our rebellious nature, takes control of our lives by his Spirit and is our Friend for all eternity. He said, 'Come to me, all whose work is hard, whose load is heavy, and I will give you rest.'[8]

2 The Creed

Q Let's turn to what the disciples of Jesus believe.
The faith into which we were baptized is summarised in the Apostles' Creed.
Please recite it now.

A I believe in God, the Father almighty,
creator of heaven and earth.
I believe in Jesus Christ, his only Son, our Lord.
He was conceived by the power of the Holy Spirit
and born of the Virgin Mary.
He suffered under Pontius Pilate,
was crucified, died, and was buried.
He descended to the dead.
On the third day he rose again.
He ascended into heaven
and is seated at the right hand of the Father.
He will come again to judge the living and the dead.
I believe in the Holy Spirit,
the holy catholic Church,
the communion of saints,
the forgiveness of sins,
the resurrection of the body
and the life everlasting.
Amen.

Q What do we mean by saying, 'I believe'?

A It means that we not only believe certain facts to be true and also that we put our whole trust in God.

Q What are the main differences between the two creeds frequently used in worship?

A The Apostles' Creed is a personal statement of baptismal faith and commitment. The Nicene Creed is longer and is a summary of the faith of the universal Church, focussed on affirming who Jesus Christ is.

Q What do we declare in the creeds?

A We believe in one God, Father, Son, and Holy Spirit, who is the creator and ruler of the universe, and has made all things for his glory.[9] Sometimes we use the word 'Trinity' to describe God.

Q What does the Church teach about God the Father?

A We believe in God the Father, source of all being and life, the one for whom we exist, who loves us and provides us with what we need for our lives, and who sent his Son to reconcile the world to himself.[10]

Q What does the Church teach about God the Son?

A We believe in God the Son, the living Word of God, the Lord of creation, who became a man and died for our sins. Our Lord was raised, victorious over death, and was exalted to the throne of God where he pleads our cause, and will come again as judge and saviour.[11] 'God loved the world so much that he gave his only Son, that everyone who believes in him may not die but have eternal life.'[12]

Q What does the Church teach about God the Holy Spirit?

A We believe in God the Holy Spirit, the life-giver; who came in fullness on the Day of Pentecost; who makes Christ known in the world, helps us to pray, equips us to serve and enables us to grow in likeness to Jesus Christ.[13]

Q What does the Church teach about the community of faith?

A We believe that the Church is the fellowship of baptized believers, the holy people of God united with those who worship God in heaven; who worship, read the Bible, pray, celebrate the Sacraments and freely share God's love. It is the family of God, the body of Christ through which he continues his reconciling work.[14]

Q Tell me what the Church teaches about final justice.

A We are told in Scripture that, because God is the source of all that is just and true, we will one day give account to God for our lives; he will destroy the power of evil and welcome us into the joy of the Lord.

Q What does the Church teach about the Christian hope?

A We believe that we are forgiven sinners, that eternal life is not broken by death, that our Lord Jesus Christ will come again in glory, and that all who belong to him will one day be raised from death in a glorious body and worship God face-to-face. [15]

Q` What eternal assurance does life in Christ give?

A The New Testament teaches that 'There is nothing in death or life - nothing in all creation that can separate us from the love of God in Christ Jesus our Lord';[16] and, 'What we shall be has not yet been disclosed, but we know that when Christ appears we shall be like him, because we shall see him as he is.'[17]

3 The Commandments

The Ten Commandments

Q Now we turn to Christian behaviour.
Please recite the Ten Commandments and summarise what they mean.[18]

A First: I am the Lord your God. You shall have no other gods but me.
We should fear, love, and trust in the Lord our God with all our being and above all things.[19]

Second: You shall not make an idol of anything and worship it.
Because we love God, we put nothing and no one else in his place. God is spirit, and those who worship him must worship in spirit and in truth.[20]

Third: You shall not dishonour the name of the Lord your God.
Because we love God we should not use his name to curse, swear, or deceive, but praise him, pray to him and give thanks to him. We are called to worship God with reverence and awe.[21]

Fourth: Remember the Lord's day and keep it holy.

Because we love God we should try to keep the day of rest each week. Christ is risen from the dead[22] and we gather to worship him, listen to his word and celebrate his sacraments with the church.[23]

Fifth: Honour your father and your mother.

Because we love others we should not despise nor provoke our parents and those in authority, but love and respect them. We live as servants of God, honour all humanity, and love our Christian brothers and sisters.[24]

Sixth: You shall not commit murder.

Because we love others we should not endanger anyone's life, nor cause harm to anyone, but help and befriend all who are in need. We should make peace with anyone who has a grievance against us, and overcome evil with good.[25]

Seventh: You shall not commit adultery.

Because we love others we should lead a pure life in word and action, respecting all relationships and particularly our marriage partner, for we know that our bodies are temples of the Holy Spirit.[26]

Eighth: You shall not steal.

Because we love others we should not rob or defraud others in any way but respect their integrity, be honest in all that we do and care for those in need.[27]

Ninth: You shall not give false evidence.

Because we love others we should not tell lies nor be false to anyone; we should interpret the actions of others charitably, speak the truth in love and be willing to apologise for our mistakes.[28]

Tenth: You shall not covet the possessions of others.

Because we love others we should not be jealous of other people but be of service to them and help them, for it is more blessed to give than to receive.[29]

Q What do these Commandments teach us about our duty towards God?

A Our duty towards God is:
- to worship him as the only true God, to love, trust, and obey him, and to bring others to know him;
- to allow nothing to take his place;
- to honour him in thought, word, and deed; and
- to respect his special day for worship, prayer, his word, rest and recreation.

Q What is our duty towards other people?

A Our duty towards our neighbour is:

- to love, respect, and help our parents and family; to honour those in authority, and to fulfil all our obligations;
- to hurt no one by word or deed, to promote peace, to bear no malice, and to be generous natured;
- to be holy by the power of the Holy Spirit who dwells within us; and to be faithful in all our relationships;
- to be honest and fair in all we do; not to steal or cheat, and to seek justice for all;
- not to tell lies, slander or gossip, and never by our silence to let others be wrongly judged; and
- to be thankful and generous, not greedy or envious, and to rejoice in other people's gifts.

The Law of Love

Q Remind me of the ancient summary of the law of God:

A The first commandment is this:
'Hear, O Israel, the Lord our God is the only Lord.
You shall love the Lord your God with all your heart,
with all your soul, with all your mind,
and with all your strength.'
The second is this: 'Love your neighbour as yourself.'
There is no other commandment greater than these.
All the law and the prophets depend on these two commandments.[30]

Q Why is this summary of the commandments important?

A The inspiration for Christian life, and the whole purpose of the Church is to love God with all our being and to love other people.

Q What was the new commandment that Jesus gave us?

A The new commandment of Jesus is to love one another just as he has loved us.[31]

Q Jesus described the character of Christian discipleship in the Beatitudes.[32] Let's recite them.

Blessed are the poor in spirit,
A for theirs is the kingdom of heaven.

Q Blessed are those who mourn,
A for they shall be comforted.

Q Blessed are the meek,
A for they shall inherit the earth.

Q Blessed are those who hunger and thirst after righteousness,
A for they shall be satisfied.

Q Blessed are the merciful,
A for they shall obtain mercy.

Q Blessed are the pure in heart,
A for they shall see God.

Q Blessed are the peacemakers,
A for they shall be called children of God.

Q Blessed are those who suffer persecution for righteousness' sake,
A for theirs is the kingdom of heaven.

4 The Presence of God

Prayer and Worship

Q Now let's consider prayer, worship and the means of grace.
What is prayer?
A Prayer is God's activity in us, for God is always interested in us.
Prayer is praise, worship and thanksgiving; it is being with God all day, every day; it is an unending conversation about everything that concerns us.
Prayer is being totally honest in God's presence; it is when God rescues us from the brink of trouble or need.
Prayer is dreaming about the future and searching for God's will; sometimes it is waiting when God seems long in coming.

Q Please recite the Lord's Prayer.[33]

A *A traditional version:*

Our Father, who art in heaven,
hallowed be thy name;
thy kingdom come;
thy will be done;
on earth as it is in heaven.
Give us this day our daily bread.
And forgive us our trespasses
as we forgive those
  who trespass against us.
And lead us not into temptation;
but deliver us from evil.
For thine is the kingdom,
the power, and the glory,
for ever and ever.
Amen.

The international version:

Our Father in heaven,
hallowed be your name,
your kingdom come,
your will be done
on earth as in heaven.
Give us today our daily bread.
Forgive us our sins
as we forgive those
  who sin against us.
Save us from the time of trial,
and deliver us from evil.*
For the kingdom, the power
and the glory are yours,
now and for ever.
Amen.

* *The Church of England altered these lines to*
'Lead us not into temptation,
but deliver us from evil.'

Q What are we taught in the Lord's Prayer?

A We are taught ...

- To pray for God to be honoured, his kingdom to come and his will be done here on earth just as it is in heaven.
- To pray for enough to meet our material and spiritual needs, and to be willing to leave the future in God's hands.
- To pray for our own forgiveness to the same extent that we forgive others.
- To pray for salvation from trials and persecution, from evil in ourselves and others; and to pray for those who suffer.
- To acknowledge that all authority, power and honour is God's, now and for ever.

Q What do we mean by worship?

A To worship God is to acknowledge his almighty power and love, to put him first in everything and to live for his honour and glory. In worship with the Church we respond to his love in praise, thanksgiving, intercession, hearing his holy word and celebrating the sacraments.

Q Can we worship alone?

A Yes, of course, because worship can take place at any time and in any place, but whenever it is possible we join with others. We are each like the broken pieces of a single loaf and belong together.[34]

Q Why does the Church keep Sunday as the usual day for worship?

A Sunday is the chief day of public worship because it was on the first day of the week that our Lord Jesus Christ rose from the dead.

Q We often share the peace during worship. Why do we do that?

A 'Peace' is an ancient word meaning 'freedom to flourish'. We share it, often with a physical sign, to demonstrate reconciliation and our love for one another.

To the One who sits on the throne and to the Lamb
be blessing and honour and glory and might,
for ever and ever. Amen.[35]

The Bible

Q What is the Bible?

A The Bible is a library of books of different kinds, divided into the Old Testament, sometimes known as the Hebrew Scriptures, and the New Testament. As a whole it is the account of God's revelation of himself to us through his ancient people of Israel, and above all in his Son, Jesus Christ.

Q Tell me more about the Bible.

A There are 66 books: 39 in the Old Testament and 27 in the New, together with some additional books in what we call The Apocrypha. Some Hebrew books are about God's law, others are history, poetry, prophecy or wise counsel. The New Testament consists of four Gospels, the Acts of the Apostles, a collection of letters from apostolic sources, and The Revelation.

Q What do Christians believe about the Scriptures?

A They are the works of authors whom we believe to have been inspired by the Holy Spirit. The Church was guided to accept the reliability of what is affirmed in these books; each has to be understood in its own time and for the kind of writing that it is.

Q How and why do we read the Bible?

A We should read the Bible regularly, praying that through it God will speak to us by his Holy Spirit, enable us to know him and do his will, and accomplish his purpose of salvation. The Christian Scriptures are the supreme guide to faith and practice, so we sometimes refer to them as the Word of the Lord.

Grace and the Sacraments

Q What do we mean by the grace of God?

A The grace of God is his free and undeserved love towards us, not accounting for our sins or our achievements of any kind. Grace is God's love in action, forgiving, inspiring and strengthening us, despite the weakness of our love for him.[36]

Q How do we receive the gifts of grace?

A We receive God's grace in the gift of each new day, in the worship and fellowship of the Church, in prayer and Bible-reading, when we receive the Sacraments, through the lives of other people, and as we seek to live to his glory.

Q Tell me what the word 'sacrament' means.

A A sacrament is an action that uses material things as signs and promises of God's grace towards us. A handshake and a kiss are sacramental acts. There are two aspects to a sacrament: the outward sign that we can experience with our senses, and the inward spiritual action of God's grace.

Q How many sacraments are there?

A There are two Sacraments of the Gospel instituted by Christ himself for fulness of life in his Church: Baptism and Holy Communion. In addition, there are sacramental actions such as confirmation, ordination, marriage, reconciliation and healing.

Q We spoke earlier of the meaning of baptism, which is where we began as Christian disciples.

What is the outward sign of baptism?

A The sign in baptism is water in which a person is baptized in the Name of the Father, and of the Son, and of the Holy Spirit.[37]

Q What is the inward spiritual gift in baptism?

A In baptism our heavenly Father sets his people free from the power of sin and death by uniting us to the death and resurrection of our Lord Jesus Christ.[38]

Q So baptism isn't just about individuals?

A No, it isn't. By water and the Holy Spirit we are reborn as the children of God and inheritors of the kingdom of heaven.[39]

Q Did baptism make you a full member of the Church?

A Yes. We are baptized into Christ and join the company of Jesus' disciples, members of his body.[40]

Q Why may children be baptized, though they are too young to speak for themselves?

A Infants are baptized because their parents and godparents claim their adoption as sons and daughters of God's covenant, heirs of his promise, and make important promises on their behalf.[41]

Q What are the outward signs in Holy Communion?

A The outward signs are bread and wine, shared at the Lord's Table, following Christ's example and obeying his command to 'Do this in remembrance of me' until he comes again.[42]

Q What is the inward spiritual gift in this sacrament?

A In the Eucharist we bring to mind his death, we celebrate his presence among us and we feed on his body and blood by faith with thanksgiving. By the act of blessing and receiving bread and wine, we are assured that we are forgiven and united to Christ.

Q What gifts do we receive in Holy Communion?

A We receive the life of Christ crucified and risen, our faith is strengthened, and we are united with the whole Church as we look forward to God's promised banquet in heaven.

Q In what spirit should we approach the Eucharist?

A We come genuinely sorry for our sins and asking for strength to live holy lives; by his grace we come joyfully reconciled to God and our neighbours; and we come ready to lead a new, better life. We pray, 'We are not worthy so much as to gather up the crumbs under your table, but you are the same Lord, whose nature is always to have mercy.'

Q What other names are given to Holy Communion?

A Holy Communion is sometimes called The Eucharist, The Lord's Supper, The Breaking of Bread or The Mass.

Q What is a rule of life?

A It is a response to God in which we commit ourselves to live each day by the power of the Spirit as disciples of Jesus Christ.

Q What should we consider for a rule of life?

A We should consider each of these:
- Praying and listening to the voice of God, worshipping with the church and being fed by him in Holy Communion.
- Growing in our knowledge of God by Bible reading, reflecting and learning.
- Witnessing to the good news of God's love in Christ by word and deed.
- Serving God and our neighbours in our daily life and work.
- Sharing God's gifts of time, talents and money with the church, our neighbours, the community and the world.

The Church

Q What are the four main characteristics of the Church?

A The Church is one, holy, catholic, and apostolic.

Q What do you mean by these words?

A The Church is one because, in spite of divisions, it is one community under one Father, whose purpose is to unite all people in Jesus Christ;

it is holy because it is set apart by God for himself, through the Holy Spirit, and is called to holy living;

it is catholic because it is universal and connected, for all nationalities and all time, holding the Christian faith in its fulness;

it is apostolic because it is sent to preach the Gospel to the whole world, and receives its teaching and authority from Christ through the Apostles' witness, the New Testament.

Q What is the Church for?

A There are three main purposes of the Church: to worship, love and serve God; to love and serve our neighbour; and, for ourselves, to enable us to grow in grace and daily increase in faith, love and obedience to God's will. The Bible calls the Church a 'spiritual temple ... a chosen race, a royal priesthood, a dedicated nation, a people claimed by God for his own, to proclaim the glorious deeds of him who has called us out of darkness into his marvellous light'.[43]

Q What is the ministry of the Church?

A Ministers are disciples who have been called by God as ambassadors for Christ and envoys of the Church. Their call has been tested by the Church, they have been trained and commissioned, and they are accountable for the ministry entrusted to them.

Conclusion

Q You have answered well. Take all this to heart and remind yourself of this teaching.

'I pray that your love may grow ever richer in knowledge and insight of every kind, enabling you to learn by experience what things really matter. Then on the day of Christ you will be flawless and without blame, yielding the full harvest of righteousness that comes through Jesus Christ, to the glory and praise of God.'[44]

A 'I am not ashamed of the gospel; it is the power of God for everyone who has faith.'[45]

Eternal God,
the light of the minds that know you,
the joy of the hearts that love you,
and the strength of the wills that serve you:
grant us so to know you that we may truly love you,
and so to love you that we may fully serve you,
whose service is perfect freedom
in Jesus Christ our Lord.

(St Augustine the African)

**Glory to the Father and to the Son and to the Holy Spirit;
as it was in the beginning, is now, and shall be for ever.
Amen.**

References

1. Genesis chapters 1, 2
2. Genesis ch 3.
3. 1 Corinthians 12. 2, 3.
4. Luke 15. 11-32
5. Romans 3. 23, 24; 1 John 1. 8, 9
6. 1 Timothy 1. 15.
7. 1 John 2. 1.
8. Matthew 11. 28.
9. Psalm 100. 3.
10. Genesis 1, 2; John 1. 1-4.
11. John 3. 16; Philippians 2. 6-11; Luke 1. 34, 35; John chs 18-20; 1 Corinthians 15. 12-14; Revelation 1. 17, 18; Hebrews 4. 14-16; 10. 19, 20; 2 Peter 3. 12, 13.
12. John 3. 16.
13. John 14. 26; 20. 21, 22; Acts 1. 4, 5; Acts ch 2; Romans 8. 9-17; 2 Corinthians 3. 18; Galatians 5. 22, 23.
14. Ephesians 4. 3-5; 1 Corinthians 12. 27; John 17. 20, 21.
15. Luke 23. 33, 34; 1 Corinthians 15. 37, 38, 42-44; John 5. 24; 11. 25, 26; Revelation 21 .3, 4.
16. Romans 8. 38, 39.
17. 1 John 3. 2.
18. Exodus 20. 1-17.
19. Matthew 22. 37; Mark 12. 30; Luke 10. 27.
20. John 4. 24.
21. Hebrews 12. 28.
22. 1 Corinthians 15. 20.
23. Acts 20. 7; 1 Corinthians 16. 2.
24. 1 Peter 2. 16, 17; John 15. 12; 1 John 3. 14; 4. 11.
25. Matthew 5. 23, 24; Colossians 3. 13.
26. 1 Corinthians 6. 19, 20; Romans 12. 21.
27. Romans 12. 1; Titus 3. 14.
28. Ephesians 4. 15.
29. Acts 20. 35.
30. Leviticus 19. 18; Deuteronomy 6. 4; Matthew 22. 37; Mark 12. 30; Luke 10. 27.
31. John 13. 34; 1 John 4 .7-11.
32. Matthew 5. 3-10.
33. Matthew 6. 9-13; Luke 11. 1-4.
34. 1 Corinthians 10. 16, 17; Hebrews 10. 25
35. Revelation 5. 13.

36. John 1. 16; Romans 3. 23; 1 John 4. 10, 19.
37. Matthew 28. 18-20.
38. Romans 6. 1-11; Colossians 2. 12.
39. John 3. 1-17
40. 1 Corinthians 12. 27
41. 1 Corinthians 7. 14
42. Matthew 26. 26-30; Mark 14. 22-25; Luke 22. 14-20; 1 Corinthians 10. 16, 17; 11. 17-34.
43. 1 Peter 2. 5, 9; Revelation 5. 10.
44. Philippians 1. 9-11.
45. Romans 1. 16.

11 Called to Pray

A form for Daily Prayer

*When more than one person use this outline, the words in normal type may be spoken by one, and the words in **bold** may be spoken by others.*

Praise

An invocation of praise may be used.

Blessèd be God: Father, Son and Holy Spirit.
Blessèd be God for ever!

Psalm

Concluding:
... **Glory to the Father, and to the Son, and to the Holy Spirit;**
   as it was in the beginning, is now, and shall be for ever. Amen.

Bible reading

Followed by a pause for reflection

A Canticle

In the morning

Benedictus / The Song of Zechariah   *Luke 1. 68-79*

Blessed be the Lord the God of Israel,
who has come to his people and set them free.
He has raised up for us a mighty Saviour,
born of the house of his servant David.
Through his holy prophets God promised of old
to save us from our enemies, from the hands of all that hate us,

To show mercy to our ancestors,
and to remember his holy covenant.
This was the oath God swore to our father Abraham:
to set us free from the hands of our enemies,
Free to worship him without fear,
holy and righteous in his sight
all the days of our life.
And you, child, shall be called the prophet of the Most High,
for you will go before the Lord to prepare his way,
To give his people knowledge of salvation
by the forgiveness of all their sins.
In the tender compassion of our God
the dawn from on high shall break upon us,
To shine on those who dwell in darkness and the shadow of death,
and to guide our feet into the way of peace.
Glory ...

Or A Song of Ezekiel   *Ezekiel 36. 24-6, 28b*

I will take you from the nations,
and gather you from all the countries.
I will sprinkle clean water upon you,
and you shall be clean from all your uncleanness.
A new heart I will give you,
and put a new spirit within you;
and I will remove from your body the heart of stone
and give you a heart of flesh.
You shall be my people, and I will be your God.
Glory ...

Or The Song of Christ's glory   *Philippians 2. 6-11*

Christ Jesus was in the form of God,
but he did not cling to equality with God.
He emptied himself, taking the form of a servant,
and was born in our human likeness.
Being found in human form he humbled himself,
and became obedient unto death, even death on a cross.

Therefore God has highly exalted him,
and bestowed on him the name above every name,
That at the name of Jesus every knee should bow,
in heaven and on earth and under the earth;
and every tongue confess that Jesus Christ is Lord,
to the glory of God the Father.
Glory ...

In the evening

Magnificat / The Song of Mary   *Luke 1. 46-55*

My soul proclaims the greatness of the Lord,
 my spirit rejoices in God my Saviour;
he has looked with favour on his lowly servant.
From this day all generations will call me blessed;
the Almighty has done great things for me and holy is his name.
He has mercy on those who fear him,
from generation to generation.
He has shown strength with his arm
and has scattered the proud in their conceit,
casting down the mighty from their thrones
and lifting up the lowly.
He has filled the hungry with good things
and sent the rich away empty.
He has come to the aid of his servant Israel,
to remember his promise of mercy,
the promise made to our ancestors,
to Abraham and his children for ever.
Glory ...

Or A Song of Deliverance   *Isaiah 12. 2-6*

Behold, God is my salvation;
I will trust and will not be afraid;
For the Lord God is my strength and my song,
and has become my salvation.
With joy you will draw water
from the wells of salvation.

On that day you will say,
'Give thanks to the Lord, call upon his name;
make known his deeds among the nations,
proclaim that his name is exalted.
Sing God's praises, who has triumphed gloriously;
let this be known in all the world.
Shout and sing for joy, you that dwell in Zion,
for great in your midst is the Holy One of Israel.
Glory ...

Or *The Beatitudes*   *Matthew 5. 3-12*

Blessed are the poor in spirit,
for theirs is the kingdom of heaven.
Blessed are those who mourn,
for they shall be comforted.
Blessed are the meek,
for they shall inherit the earth.
Blessed are those who hunger
and thirst after righteousness,
for they shall be satisfied.
Blessed are the merciful,
for they shall obtain mercy.
Blessed are the pure in heart,
for they shall see God.
Blessed are the peacemakers,
for they shall be called children of God.
Blessed are those who suffer persecution for righteousness' sake,
for theirs is the kingdom of heaven.
Glory ...

At night

Nunc Dimittis / Song of Simeon   *Luke 2. 29-32*

Now, Lord, you let your servant go in peace:
your word has been fulfilled.
My own eyes have seen the salvation
which you have prepared in the sight of every people;

a light to reveal you to the nations
and the glory of your people Israel.
Glory ...

Prayer

Give thanks and pray for
* the gift of today
* the world and its needs
* the Church and her life
* the community and all who serve people in need
* your life offered to God

The prayers may conclude with the collect of the day **or**

In the morning

Lord God of all creation,
we offer you the life of this new day:
give us grace to love and serve you
to the praise of Jesus Christ our Lord.
Amen.

In the evening

Eternal Lord, our beginning and our end:
bring us with the whole creation to your glory,
hidden through past ages
and made known in Jesus Christ our Lord.
Amen.

At night

Be present, O merciful God,
and protect us through the silent hours of this night,
so that we who are wearied
   by the changes and chances of this fleeting world,
may rest upon your eternal changelessness;
through Jesus Christ our Lord.
Amen.

Our Father ...

Ending

Either

The Lord bless us
and preserve us from all evil
and keep us in eternal life.
Amen.

Or

**The grace of our Lord Jesus Christ,
and the love of God,
and the fellowship of the Holy Spirit
be with us all evermore.
Amen.**

And

Let us bless the Lord.
Thanks be to God.

Some material is Copyright © The Archbishops' Council of the Church of England, 2000-2006

26567307R00093

Printed in Great Britain
by Amazon